Diversity of Capitalism in Central and Eastern Europe

Eric Magnin · Nikolay Nenovsky

Diversity of Capitalism in Central and Eastern Europe

Dependent Economies and Monetary Regimes

palgrave
macmillan

Eric Magnin
LADYSS, Department of Economics
University Paris Cité
Paris, France

Nikolay Nenovsky
LEFMI, Department of Economics
University of Picardie Jules Verne
Amiens, France

Department of Theoretical Economy
State University HSE
and Department of Political
Economy, RUDN
Moscow, Russia

ISBN 978-3-031-04949-1 ISBN 978-3-031-04950-7 (eBook)
https://doi.org/10.1007/978-3-031-04950-7

This Palgrave Macmillan imprint is published by the registered company Springer Nature Switzerland AG
The registered company address is: Gewerbestrasse 11, 6330 Cham, Switzerland

Acknowledgements

This book would probably never have been written without the leadership and coordination by Prof. Xavier Richet, from Sorbonne Nouvelle University, of a European research program (Jean Monnet), *Multidisciplinary Perspectives on the European Integration of the Western Balkans* (BALKINT, 2013–2016). The question of the emergence of dependent capitalism in the countries of Central and Eastern Europe and the Balkans in particular was one of the key issues of the program, which led to several scientific conferences in the Balkan countries. This program has stimulated us to develop further our research in this field. We would like to pay tribute to and warmly thank Prof. Xavier Richet, a tireless traveller and distinguished scholar, who left us prematurely at the beginning of the year 2022. We have lost a teacher, a colleague appreciated by all, of great generosity, and a friend. We dedicate to him these few pages devoted to a part of Europe, of which he knew the smallest corners and was able to analyse the upheavals.

Contents

List of Figures

List of Tables

CHAPTER 1

Introduction

Abstract Since the beginning of the 1990s, the literature devoted to the diversity of capitalism models around the world has considerably expanded. The systemic transformation in Central and Eastern Europe, following the fall of the Berlin Wall, has contributed to this development. The 2008 financial crisis revealed the fragilities of CEE countries and led some authors to propose the concept of "dependent capitalism" to refer to these economies. The aim of this book is to question the relevance of this assumption and to specify, within an institutionalist theoretical framework, the characteristics of this emergent economic model, its strengths and weaknesses, its genesis and its capacity to endure crises and persist through time. The dependent monetary regime appears to be a key institution of this type of capitalism, consistent with the other institutional forms that define this configuration.

Keywords Comparative capitalism · Comparative economic systems · French *Régulation* School · Dependent capitalism · Dependent monetary regime · Monetary sovereignty

E. Magnin and N. Nenovsky, *Diversity of Capitalism in Central and Eastern Europe*, https://doi.org/10.1007/978-3-031-04950-7_1

Since the beginning of the 1990s, the literature devoted to the diversity of capitalism models around the world has considerably expanded. The systemic transformation in Central and Eastern Europe, following the fall of the Berlin Wall, has contributed to this development for several reasons. First of all, it requires considering ex ante the question of the outcomes of these changes, i.e. the transition to what. The standard answer was that of a "transition to a market economy". But for many specialists, this was considered too vague and theoretical, and poorly reflecting the reality of developed countries with their variety of national forms of capitalism. Second, institutional changes since 1990 have raised questions about emerging economic models as a result of these transformations. Third, the fall of the Wall has, according to Albert (1993), sealed the victory of "capitalism" and shifted the rivalry opposing the two great families of systems, capitalism and socialism, to a competition among several varieties of capitalism in the context of globalization. Finally, research development on the diversity of capitalisms since the 1990s would not have been possible without the acknowledgement and development of the institutional approach in economics, itself stimulated by the lessons of the transition (EBRD, 1999; UNECE, 1999; World Bank, 2002, 2005).

Comparative Capitalism (CC) is rooted in a dual tradition, which it both extends and renews, comparative economic systems (CES) and comparative institutional analysis. The boundaries between these approaches are by no means impermeable, since the former gives a central place to institutions[1] and the latter is focused on the diversity of national institutional configurations over time and space. The modern version of CES was born with the first debates of the 1920s and 1930s on the rationality of a planned economy between O. Lange, L. von Mises and F. Hayek (Hayek, 1935).[2] It reached its peak in the 1970s with the work of Holesovsky (1977), Koopmans and Montias (1971) and Duffy and Neuberger (1976). At that time, the aim was essentially to compare the two great economic systems that faced each other: the socialist system

[1] «The field of comparative economic system is primarily concerned with the study of economic institutions, emphasizing the influence of these institutions on the performance of an economy.» (Conn, 1978, p. 355) However, the use of institutions can fall within a neoclassical (neoinstitutionalist) or an old institutionalist framework.

[2] CES's origins go back further. Although there are some earlier works, Marx makes an important contribution to the field with his idea of a succession of modes of production throughout history (Lane, 2005). On the emergence and development of comparative economic systems as a branch of economics, see Conn (1978) and Neuberger (1984).

of the former USSR and its Eastern European or Chinese versions, and Western capitalism. It is not surprising in these conditions that the demise of the socialist system in Europe led to the disappearance of comparative analysis of economic systems. The second approach developed in the 1960s following the work of Shonfield (1965) and of the French *Régulation*[3] School from the 1970s onwards. In this latter framework, capitalism is defined, at a high level of abstraction, as a mode of production, where market relations and an essentially conflictual capital/labour relationship dominate. But beyond the Marxian influence appears the idea of a diversity in time and space of fundamental social relationships, codified in institutional forms, within the same mode of production. They are likely to sustain a regime of accumulation via a mode of *régulation* that ensures the reproduction of these fundamental social relationships over time (Boyer 1990). Comparative capitalism was initially concerned with Western developed countries. Since the 1990s, this field of research has been extended to emerging, transitional and/or developing countries (Schedelik et al., 2021). The present book is devoted to the diversity of capitalism in Central and Eastern Europe including Baltic countries and the Balkans, with a specific focus on monetary regimes.

Actually, the 2008 financial crisis revealed the fragilities of Central and Eastern European (CEE) countries and led some authors to propose the concept of "dependent capitalism" to refer to these economies (King 2002, Nölke & Vliegenthart, 2009), an assumption that has become relevant for many scholars (Chepurenko & Szanyi, 2021). Dependency is an old idea, generally referring to the 1960s–1970s work on development in Latin America within a Marxist theoretical framework (Evans, 1979). The aim here is not to revive these approaches but to revisit the concept in the field of Comparative Capitalism, in a very different theoretical and historical context. However, we rely on a critical version of CC, combining the VoC (Varieties of Capitalism) approach, international political economy and *Régulation* theory, with an emphasis on power relationships, alliances and conflicts between internal and external actors and asymmetric interactions between national models of capitalism (May & Nölke, 2018). In this respect, dependence is not the same as interdependence. All countries or almost all countries are interdependent in a globalized world. But dependence implies the existence of asymmetric relations between

[3] The word *régulation*, which here means regulation of a system, is written in French with an *é* so as not to confuse it with the English word regulation (in the sense of rules).

internal and external actors. Generally speaking, dependence means that growth and capital accumulation depend on economic decisions taken by actors outside the country. The main feature of dependent capitalism is dependence on foreign capital. The need for external capital is dictated by insufficient domestic savings, and a generally low technological level and limited competitive export opportunities. This dependence also presupposes unfavourable power relations, which means that external actors with capital (multinational firms, international organizations, etc.) are likely to impose institutional changes that will serve their interests. Dependence generally results in capturing value for the benefit of external economic actors. However, the present perspective on dependence is not intended to be normative, and dependence is not a priori considered negative. Under certain conditions, dependent capitalism may appear as a relatively successful model and be a step towards gaining more independence, as the developed economies of East Asia have demonstrated.

The concept of dependent capitalism means that we are considering a «model», an ideal-type, consisting of a set of complementary institutions, which reinforce each other and give the economic model a relative stability over time, likely to sustain a more or less virtuous growth dynamics. The monetary regime is one of these key institutions that contribute to the coherence of the whole. Though not much studied in the literature on CC—because of its focus on VoC—it appears to be an essential element of the institutional configurations of dependent economies. In the CEE countries and especially in the Balkans, institutional changes since 1990 have led to the emergence of dependent monetary regimes, the extreme forms of which being Currency boards and euroization (Magnin & Nenovsky, 2021). Historically, this monetary dependence is older and its path can be traced back to the nineteenth century and the Latin Monetary Union (Nenovsky & Vaslin, 2020) and in a long historical perspective to this day (Magnin & Nenovsky, 2022; Olszak, 1996; Pecorari, 2006).

Dependent monetary regimes constrain the economic monetary sovereignty of a country, both in its domestic dimension—monetary policy—and in terms of the exchange rate regime (Zimmermann, 2013). In varying degrees according to the form of the monetary regime, i.e. according to the degree of its dependence, these countries lose their monetary instruments as well as the ability to influence the monetary base and therefore the money supply and the real economy. Monetary and exchange rate policies passively follow the monetary and exchange rate policies of the country (currency area) chosen as an external anchor. Domestic sources of money creation are severely contracted or absent, and the money supply becomes highly or completely dependent on balance of payments dynamics.

The function of Lender of Last Resort (LOLR) is limited, as is the capacity to respond to a systemic crisis. The volumes of money income, seigniorage, are also insignificant. Hard constraints are also placed on fiscal policy, the budget must be balanced and public debts low. Failure to exercise fiscal discipline and the existence of an inflexible labour market (and when wages grow faster than labour productivity) threaten the very existence of the chosen dependent, passive monetary regime. All of the features listed so far resemble in many respects the operation of the gold and gold-exchange standards (Desquilbet & Nenovsky, 2004). Similar to the gold standard and gold-exchange standard, it is argued that modern dependent monetary regimes, by delegating monetary authority externally, provide creditworthiness and credibility in currency, of course at the expense of losing monetary flexibility. It is argued that the choice of a dependent monetary regime is successful when the benefits are greater than the losses, both statically and dynamically.

The present book intends to address the following questions. What type/variety of capitalism is emerging as a result of the socio-economic transformations achieved in the CEE and Balkan countries since 1990? Shall we really refer to it as a "model"? If so, is it unique or multiple? Is the concept of dependent capitalism relevant to describe this model? What are its main characteristics, strengths and weaknesses? Is the macroeconomic dynamic sustainable, virtuous, and is the model viable on the long term given the different crises it has faced (2008 financial crisis, COVID-19 pandemic)? What is the contribution of monetary regimes to the overall configuration and evolution of these economies?

Regarding the monetary regime, we will try to answer on the basis of the theory and the practice of the four selected "extremely dependent monetary regimes" (two Currency Boards—Bulgaria and Bosnia and Herzegovina—and two euroizations—Montenegro and Kosovo), how and why they were introduced, to what extent are they the country's own choice and to what extent are they imposed by external economic and geopolitical interests? How do dependent money regimes fit into and alter the overall institutional configuration of dependent capitalism, especially conservative finance and the liberal labour market? To what extent do dependent monetary regimes facilitate the attraction of foreign capital and foreign direct investment (FDI), as well as foreign financial, especially banking institutions.

According to proponents of dependent regimes, the loss of discretion is insignificant compared to the benefits associated with monetary stability and low exchange rate risk premium, which generally help attract foreign capital. Foreign capital together with low interest rates and inflation in turn provides growth and high employment. It is hoped this will allow the economy to move towards high-technology production areas within global value chains. There is also an interesting question about the response of dependent monetary regimes in a crisis, and especially in a systemic one. The crisis that began in 2008 and affected the European Union (EU) peripheral countries and the euro area, and the pandemic crisis that followed in 2020 provide an opportunity to test the resilience of dependent monetary regimes.

To explore these issues, the first part of the book takes a theoretical perspective and presents in Chapter 2 the two main approaches to comparative capitalism and their application to post-socialist CEE countries, before putting the model of dependent capitalism back into the debates on dependency and into a new theoretical and historical context (Chapter 3). Chapter 4 explains the concept of a dependent monetary regime and the different institutional arrangements it encompasses. The second part, more empirical, studies in Chapter 5 the various national trajectories in Central and Eastern Europe and the Balkans and shows how dependent capitalism gradually emerged during the years 1990–2000 and the role of the former socialist system's legacy in this evolution. It also brings to light in Chapters 6 and 7 the specificities of dependent monetary regimes implemented in some Balkan countries, namely Currency boards or the development of euroization.

This is one of the first comprehensive studies of dependent money regimes within the concept of dependent capitalism. Our modest ambition is to benefit students and researchers, as well as all those who are interested in the regimes and the countries of Central and Eastern Europe, especially the Balkans.

References

Albert, M. (1993). *Capitalism against capitalism*. Whurr Publishers.

Boyer, R. (1990). *The régulation school: A critical introduction*. Columbia University Press.

Chepurenko, A., & Szanyi, M. (2021). *Parallel processes and divergent outcomes: The transformation of the economies of former socialist countries* (Leibniz Institut für Ost und Südosteuropaforschung Working Papers No. 393).

Conn, D. (1978). Economic theory and comparative economic systems: A partial literature survey. *Journal of Comparative Economics, 2*(3), 355–381.

Desquilbet, J. B., & Nenovsky, N. (2005). Confiance et ajustement dans les régimes de caisse d'émission. *Monde En Développement, 2*(130), 77–95.

Duffy, W., & Neuberger, E. (1976). *Comparative economic systems: A decision-making approach.* Allyn and Bacon.

EBRD. (1999). *Transition report: Ten years of transition.* European Bank for Reconstruction and Development.

Evans, P. (1979). *Dependent development: The alliance of multinational, state, and local capital in Brazil.* Princeton University Press.

Hayek, F. (Ed.). (1935). *Collectivist economic planning.* Routledge & Kegan Paul.

Holesovsky, V. (1977). *Economic systems: Analysis and comparison.* McGraw-Hill.

King, L. (2002). Postcommunist divergence: A comparative analysis of the transition to capitalism in Poland and Russia. *Studies in Comparative International Development, 37*(3), 3–34.

Koopmans, T., & Montias, J. (1971). On the description and comparison of economic systems. In A. Eckstein (Ed.), *Comparison of economic systems. Theoretical and methodological approaches* (pp. 27–78). University of California Press.

Lane, D. (2005). Emerging varieties of capitalism in former state socialist societies. *Competition and Change, 9*(3), 227–247.

Magnin, E., & Nenovsky, N. (2021). Dependent monetary regimes in the Balkans: Enlarging the "varieties of capitalism" hypothesis. *International Journal of Public Administration, 44*(14), 1216–1230.

Magnin, E., & Nenovsky, N. (2022). Balkan monetary dependence during the XIXth and XXth centuries. *Economic Alternatives,* (2), 171–200.

May, C., & Nölke, A. (2018). Dangers of residual dependency in state-permeated capitalism: The case of Brazil during labor party rule. *Revue De La Régulation, 24*(2), 1–24.

Nenovsky, N., & Vaslin, J. M. (2020). Shadowing the Latin monetary union: Monetary regimes and interest rates at the Balkans periphery (1867–1912). *The Journal of European Economic History, 23*(2), 71–114.

Neuberger, E. (1984). Systèmes économiques comparés, vue d'ensemble. In D. Greenwald (Ed.), *Encyclopédie Économique* (pp. 953–959). Economica.

Nölke, A., & Vliegenthart, A. (2009). Enlarging the variety of capitalism. The emergence of dependent market economies in East Central Europe. *World Politics, 61*(4), 670–702.

Olszak, N. (1996). *Histoire des unions monétaires*. Presses Universitaires fr France.

Pecorari, P. (2006). La Banca Nazionale di Romania et il problema degli utili netti nel 1913. In P. Pecorari (Ed.), *La lira debole. L'Italia, l'Unione Monetaria Latina et il "bimetallismo zoppo"* (pp. 201–226). CEDAM.

Schedelik, M., Nölke, A., Mertens, D., & May, C. (2021). Comparative capitalism, growth models and emerging markets: The development of the field. *New Political Economy, 26*(4), 514–526.

Shonfield, A. (1965). *Modern capitalism: The changing balance of public and private power*. Oxford University Press.

UNECE. (1999). *Economic survey of Europe 1999* (N°1). United Nations Economic Commission for Europe.

World Bank. (2002). *Building institutions for markets* (World Development Report 2002). Oxford University Press.

World Bank. (2005). *Economic growth in the 1990s: Learning from a decade of reform*. World Bank.

Zimmermann, C. (2013). The concept of monetary sovereignty revisited. *The European Journal of International Law, 24*(3), 797–818.

PART I

Theoretical Foundations

CHAPTER 2

Varieties or Diversity of Capitalism?

Abstract This chapter presents the field of Comparative Capitalism (CC) and its relevance for Central and Eastern European countries (CEECs) since the 1990s. Two main approaches stand out in the abundance of work on this topic in the recent period: *varieties of capitalisms* (VoC), proposed by Hall and Soskice (*Varieties of capitalism: The institutional foundations of comparative advantage*. Oxford University Press, 2001), and *diversity of capitalism*, which falls within the French School of *Régulation*, promoted by Amable (*The diversity of modern capitalism*. Oxford University Press, 2003) and Boyer (*The regulation school: A critical introduction*. Columbia University Press, 1990). Amable criticizes the binary vision of the VoC and opts for a typology that identifies five models of capitalism. In the recent period, CC has been considerably enriched by integrating the concepts of institutional complementarity and hierarchy. The post-socialist transformation is a privileged field of application for CC and contributes to its renewal. Most of the work focusing on CEECs can be grouped according to their proximity to both approaches. However, some authors have developed their own typologies, considering that these two main approaches are not adapted to transition countries.

Keywords Comparative capitalism · Varieties of Capitalism (VoC) · Diversity of capitalism · Institutional complementarity · Institutional hierarchy · *Régulation* theory · Central and Eastern Europe

E. Magnin and N. Nenovsky, *Diversity of Capitalism in Central and Eastern Europe*, https://doi.org/10.1007/978-3-031-04950-7_2

Since the early 1990s, a vast literature has contributed to expanding the field of Comparative Capitalism (CC). The development of this research coincides with the «transition to a market economy» in Central and Eastern European countries. Within this academic profusion, many specialists refer more or less implicitly to two major approaches, sometimes unfortunately confounded, which have gained some influence: the so-called Varieties of Capitalism approach (VoC) proposed by Hall and Soskice (2001) and the French *régulationist* approach proposed by Amable (2000, 2003, 2009), within a theoretical framework first elaborated by Boyer (1990, 1995, 1996). Since the 2000s, Comparative Capitalism has adopted new conceptual tools by successfully integrating the concepts of institutional complementarity and institutional hierarchy. While the post-socialist transformation process has helped to stimulate research on the diversity of models of capitalism, Central and Eastern European countries in turn constitute a privileged field of application for these theoretical approaches.

Two Main Approaches in Comparative Capitalism

Varieties of Capitalism

As Hall and Soskice (2001) state, the VoC approach places the firm at the centre of the analysis. The firm is indeed considered as the crucial actor of a capitalist economy whose success lies on the development and exploitation of its core competencies or «dynamic capabilities». Hall and Soskice insist on the firm's relational dimension. The firm's success largely depends on the quality of the relationships it is able to establish with internal employees and external actors, such as suppliers, customers, shareholders, unions, business associations and governments. Coordination problems are therefore at the heart of the VoC approach.

Hall and Soskice distinguish five activity spheres in which firms will have to solve coordination problems that are decisive for the exploitation and development of their core competencies: industrial relations, vocational training and education, corporate governance, interfirm relations and relations with their own employees. There are two main ways of solving these coordination problems, which differentiate the two main types of capitalism in developed economies: coordination based on market mechanisms, typical of liberal market economies (LMEs), and non-market coordination, characteristic of coordinated market economies (CMEs).

The VoC framework can be considered as a neoinstitutionalist approach, as evidenced by references to North, Williamson and Aoki (Chavance, 2008). Indeed, the concepts of formal and informal institutions, as well as the market-hierarchy dichotomy, play an important role in Hall and Soskice's work, as does the idea that institutions, whose historical dimension is emphasized, facilitate the coordination of actors' relations. Firms' strategies are themselves dependent on national institutional configurations since the latter provide a specific set of opportunities. Hence, the VoC approach expects very different firm strategies in LMEs and CMEs given their respective historically rooted institutional environment.

Germany is a textbook case of a coordinated market economy. Non-market coordination prevails in the five activity spheres. Firms' access to finance does not depend on short-term profitability criteria but, in return, investors must have access to reliable information on firms' performance. Interfirm networks, trust and reputation play a decisive role in the control and circulation of information. The company's decision-making structure based on consensus building between internal and external members encourages information sharing. Cooperation in the field of industrial relations takes the form of industry-level wage settlements between trade unions and employer associations and of firm-level working councils providing security against arbitrary layoffs and worsening working conditions. Workers are then encouraged to invest in high industry-specific or firm-specific skills and enjoy a large autonomy in their work. These skills are provided by the education and training system which is jointly managed by employer associations, trade unions and the state. Finally, inter-enterprise relations facilitate the diffusion of technology across the economy through various channels: business associations, public research institutes and industry associations capable of promoting common industrial standards and resolving disputes among firms.

The United States is the prime example of a liberal market economy where coordination problems in the different spheres are solved mainly through market relations. Firms' financing conditions depend on stock prices and hence on their ability to generate short-term profits. Industrial relations are characterized by market-based relations between individual worker and employer. The labour market is highly flexible which prompts individuals to invest in general skills, easier to transfer across different firms. The education and training system generally focus on the provision of non-specialized competencies. Interfirm relations are competitive and regulated by antitrust laws designed to prevent companies from colluding to control prices or markets. Labour market fluidity ensures technology transfer through the movement of scientists and engineers from one company to another. Industrial standards emerge from market races resulting in patent filing and commercialization for the winners.

Hall and Soskice also include in their theoretical framework the concept of «comparative institutional advantage», which proposes a renewed response to the issue of international specialization. According to them, the institutional structure of a national economy provides firms with comparative advantages for engaging in specific types of activities. As far as the innovation process is concerned, they show that CMEs' institutional features encourage specialization in industrial sectors where incremental innovation, based on the improvement of specific skills, is prevalent. On the contrary, LMEs' institutional configuration facilitates fast changes and specialization in sectors dominated by radical innovation.

The VoC approach rests on a binary classification of capitalisms into liberal market economies and coordinated market economies, which provides a clear theoretical framework to compare various national economies.[1] However, the downside lies in the reduced economic complexity it brings about by focusing on one dimension, the firm and its coordination problems, and one dividing criterion, namely market role.[2] As a result, this dichotomy cannot include all developed economies, as Hall and Soskice (2001, p. 21) themselves acknowledge by referring to the «more ambiguous positions» of some countries (France, Italy, Spain, Portugal, Greece and Turkey). These intermediate cases lead them to consider the possibility of «another type of capitalism, sometimes described as 'Mediterranean'» (idem). Since the original contribution of Hall and Soskice, the VoC approach has been enlarged to emerging and developing countries and has given rise to new varieties of capitalism: dependent market economies (DMEs) in Central and Eastern Europe (Nölke & Vliegenthart, 2009), hierarchical market economies (HMEs)

[1] This dichotomy recalls the distinction originally made by Albert (1993) between Rhenish capitalism and Anglo-Saxon capitalism.

[2] Ebenau (2012, p. 208) criticizes the VoC on three points: «(1) its problematic functionalism and firm-centrism; (2) its methodological nationalism; (3) its disregard for change and history».

in Latin America (Schneider, 2009), state-permeated market economies (SMEs) for the BRICS countries (May & Nölke, 2018) and even patrimonial market economies (PMEs) for Russia and some Arab countries (Becker & Vasileva, 2017; Schlumberger, 2008).[3]

Diversity of Capitalism

The other theoretical framework, not as influential as the previous one, which falls within Comparative Capitalism, is the one proposed by Amable in 2003. Unfortunately, a common mistake is to confuse Amable's work with the VoC approach, whereas both theoretical bases are very different (Schedelik et al., 2021). The former lies on the *Régulation* theory (RT), which can be considered as a broader macroeconomic theoretical framework developed in the 1970s to explain contemporary capitalism dynamics (growth and crisis), whereas VoC is a theoretical approach, with a rather microeconomic perspective, specifically developed to grasp the varieties of Western capitalism and their performances.[4] The diversity in time and space of national socio-economic trajectories is one of the founding issues of the Régulation theory (Boyer, 1990). Confronted to VoC's binary approach, *régulationist* authors, on the contrary, point to a diversity of forms of capitalism. Amable (2003) proposes a typology with five models.

His approach follows an international comparative study carried out by Amable et al. (1997) on social systems of innovation and production (SSIP). The notion of SSIP refers to the idea that technical change is a systemic phenomenon that goes beyond the spheres of science and technology. Innovation takes place in a specific institutional and economic context, marked by the interaction between the scientific and technical system, the education and training system, the financing system, the wage-labour nexus, the competition structure, the role of the state in the economy and the degree of international integration. It is a combination of organizational, institutional and technological factors that determine the configuration of innovations and, by extension, the growth regime. This analysis leads to identify four different SSIPs, combining

[3] For a survey on VoC models, see Feldmann (2019), Vasileva and Schmidt (2019), and Schedelik et al. (2021).

[4] For a discussion between the VoC approach and the *Régulation* theory, see Boyer (2005a).

specific innovation dynamics and configurations of institutional forms: the market-based SSIP, the meso-corporatist SSIP, the "European" SSIP and the social-democratic SSIP. This result demonstrates, for the authors, before the VoC approach, that there are more than two models beyond the LME and CME dichotomy.

Amable (2003) then proposes to take the comparative analysis of capitalism a step further by identifying a certain number of "key institutional domains" (which are actually very close to the original institutional forms of the *Régulation* school)[5] in which OECD countries show significant differences. These include competition on product markets, wage-labour nexus, financial intermediation and corporate governance, social protection and the education system. Amable supports his demonstration with a data analysis, based on the principal component analysis method coupled with an ascending hierarchical classification, of 21 OECD countries to identify five types of capitalism. The five models are: the market-based economies or the Anglo-Saxon model (United States, United Kingdom, Canada, Australia), the social-democratic economies (Sweden, Finland, Denmark), the Continental European capitalism (France, Germany, Austria, Belgium, Netherlands, Switzerland, Norway), the South European capitalism (Italy, Spain, Portugal, Greece) and Asian capitalism (Japan, South Korea). This typology seems to be consistent with other contributions to the literature on comparative capitalism (Sapir, 2005, for example). However, each model can be considered as an ideal-type, to which no real economy could perfectly apply.

The market-based model is close to the LME type since market mechanisms prevail in the different institutional fields under study. Social democratic capitalism is characterized by the high level and universal nature of social protection, cooperative industrial relations, a bank-based financial system and an active presence of the state. The continental European model is not very different, with greater employment protection and sometimes more conflictual labour relations. The Mediterranean model is characterized by a dual labour market, weaker social protection and an

[5] *Régulation* theory initially identifies five «institutional forms», defined as the codification of fundamental social relationships: monetary and financial regime, wage-labour nexus, competition conditions, State, mode of international integration. They sustain a «regime of accumulation» (Boyer, 1990). The stabilization of an accumulation regime at a given period of time is related to the emergence of a «mode of *régulation*» and its ability to adapt to change.

education system that is more focused on the acquisition of general skills. Regarding Asian capitalism, it is marked by the influence of large corporations, cooperative labour relations, weak social protection and a low level of public spending on education.

Institutional Complementarity and Hierarchy

Institutional Complementarity

Both the VoC and the diversity of capitalisms approaches share a common feature: they highlight the significance of institutional complementarity. They define it in a relatively similar way. Two institutions can be described as complementary when «the existence or the particular form taken by an institution in one area reinforces the presence, functioning or efficiency of another institution in another area» (Amable, 2003, p. 60). Both approaches acknowledge Aoki's (1994) authorship in using this concept.[6]

Amable (2003) chooses the example of the complementarity between financial system and training system to illustrate the concept. A market-based financial system encourages short-term profitability, which results, on the employment side, in a firm's low commitment to its employees with a high risk of layoffs. Under these conditions, employees will prefer to acquire general rather than firm-specific skills to facilitate their redeployment to other firms. A bank-based financial system fosters long-term investment, which in turn promotes stable trade-offs between social partners that encourage the acquisition of specific skills. In both cases, each institution reinforces the influence of the other. CMEs and LMEs' institutional characteristics presented earlier also demonstrate their complementarity.

Boyer (2005b) specifies the meaning of complementarity by emphasizing the distinction between compatibility, coherence and complementarity. Two (or more) institutions are compatible if they can be observed jointly in some countries. But this compatibility does not

[6] In his 1994 article, Aoki acknowledges the influence of Meyer et al. (1992) regarding the concept of institutional complementarity. He emphasizes the complementarity between the bank-enterprise relationship, the labour market configuration (low mobility) and a team-based organization of production in Japan's high-growth period. The concept of complementarity is also useful, according to him, for analysing transition economies. It argues for a bank-based rather than market-based financial system in these countries.

necessarily involve coherence or complementarity. Two (or more) institutions are coherent if their coexistence is justified for some reasons, especially theoretical ones. Coherence suggests a mutual strengthening of the functioning of each institution, which is a step in the direction of complementarity without necessarily reaching it. Complementarity adds to coherence a notion of higher performance resulting from the combination of these two institutions. Complementarity can therefore be understood as «a successful» coherence. The degree of adequacy of two (or more) institutions can therefore be classified in increasing order, from compatible to coherent and then complementary. Coherence adds some sense to the idea of a simple coexistence underlying the notion of compatibility. Complementarity involves enhanced performance, which requires the choice of performance criteria.

From the concept of institutional complementarity, a certain number of implications arise, some of which with systemic connotations. A model of capitalism is not a collection of institutional forms, randomly gathered, but a specific combination of these forms linked by complementarity relations. These relations ensure the coherence of the model concerned, which can be qualified as systemic. On the other hand, the complementarity-coherence relationship is not necessarily reciprocal. If we retain the distinction made by Boyer, coherence is a first step towards complementarity but cannot be identified with it.

Consequently, it becomes difficult, both theoretically and empirically, to associate economic performance with an isolated institution, given the interdependence between institutions. Actually, it is a configuration of complementary institutional forms «making a system» that is responsible for the overall performance of the model. The systemic dimension reappears here because the performance of the whole is greater than the sum of the positive effects (according to some criteria) that each institutional form taken in isolation could have produced. The definition of the performance of a model of capitalism and the choice of these performance indicators are therefore crucial here. Can GDP growth, for example, still be considered as a unique and reliable indicator, even though it is used in many econometric estimates? Moreover, a model may be assessed as performing well on the basis of some criteria (e.g. growth) but not on others (e.g. reducing inequality).

Moreover, it is neither possible nor advisable to design an optimal institutional configuration, which would combine institutions from different countries considered as the most «efficient» in each field: for example, the American labour market regulations and tax system, with the Swedish education system, with the Danish employment policy, etc. Importing into one type of capitalism an isolated institutional form from another model could lead to an unsustainable configuration. Amable (2009), for example, questions the coherence of the association between labour market flexibility and a «generous» welfare state, the famous «flexicurity». Similarly, Cernat (2006) questions the economic efficiency of the «cocktail capitalism» which is in his view emerging in the new EU Member States, a combination of institutions imported from different models. This anti-benchmarking argument is decisive for economic policy. Institutional complementarity requires complementarity both in the reforms implemented and in the choice of institutions. Inconsistent or partial structural reforms may not lead to the expected «performance target».[7] Conversely, it is easy to imagine that different combinations of complementary institutions could produce similar macroeconomic performances. This was the case with the Anglo-Saxon model and the social-democratic model in the 1990s (Aiginger, 2005). This is also the basic postulate of the VoC approach, at the root of the CME-LME dichotomy.

Institutional complementarity may also be considered as one of the sources of path dependence and lock-in phenomena (Hodgson, 1993; Magnin, 2002). As the complementary institutions of the same model reinforce each other, the model will tend to persist over time. And national trajectories will tend to be «locked» into a model or, to use a mathematical metaphor, to gravitate around a «systemic attractor», the core representing the model's «founding institutional compromise» (Boyer, 2011, p. 112).

Institutional Hierarchy

The concept of institutional hierarchy is to be found mainly in the diversity of capitalisms approach and falls within the recent *régulationist* tradition (Amable, 2003; Boyer, 2005b, 2015; Petit, 2005). It conveys

[7] Impossible not to think here of the Soviet model adopted in Eastern Europe after World War II and of the repeated failure of partial reforms implemented in various countries until the 1980s, attesting the strong coherence of the model (Chavance, 2019; Kornai, 1980). A (systemic) coherence, the strength of which raises questions about the complementarity of the underlying institutions and thus about the performances of this model.

the idea that an institutional form plays a dominant role in relation to the others at a given point in time, both in the organization of complementarity relations and in the dynamic evolution of the institutional structure. The authors recognize in the formation of this hierarchy the expression of power relations and political compromises.[8] But it is the emergent, unintended result of an unplanned process of confrontation of interests at a given point in time. For example, the primacy of the wage-labour nexus in the Fordist period is the outcome of post-war socio-political compromises. Since the 1980s, this hierarchy has been called into question with the liberal turn in favour of other institutional forms: competition conditions for some specialists and finance for others (Boyer, 2000, 2015).

The concept of institutional hierarchy also requires further comments. Institutional hierarchy and complementarity can be considered as distinct but related concepts. Indeed, one manifestation of a hierarchy lies in the influence, through constraints and incentives, that the dominant institution exerts on the modalities of complementarity within a given institutional configuration. It leads other institutions to strengthen it, even if it means making them evolve a little. For example, the priority given to workers during the Fordist period leads to the articulation of other institutional forms in such a way as to strengthen it. Or else, the predominance of finance in the recent period has led to an evolution in the wage-labour nexus and social welfare, so as to serve finance's interests.

Similarly, from a dynamic perspective, a change in the dominant institution may lead to changes in one or more other complementary institutional forms (Boyer, 2015). However, given the complementarity effects, even a localized change can affect other institutions and hence lead to more significant changes (Amable, 2003).

Among major changes, a distinction must be made between those affecting hierarchy and those affecting complementarity. The former result in a possible shift in the institutional hierarchy as a consequence of changing political power relations, but without necessarily leading to a change in the model of capitalism. The latter correspond to the case where a change in institutional forms and complementarity, without a change in hierarchy, would lead to a transition from one model to another. Finally, a

[8] The institutional hierarchy expresses the domination of a political coalition representing common interests and an agreement on a political strategy (Amable, 2003; Amable & Palombarini, 2008).

last possible case could combine both effects, for instance if a shift in hierarchy brought about a change in the model of capitalism, e.g. a hierarchy dominated by finance leading to a convergence towards Anglo-Saxon capitalism.

Comparative Capitalism could be qualified at first glance as static. But it is not. Each model of capitalism appears, admittedly, as a stylized picture at a moment t, representing a more or less large interval of time. However, the perception of a frozen model in time is above all the result of the path-dependent effects associated with the «founding institutional compromise» of each model, which is embedded in time. Still, models are constantly evolving under the action of different forces, which can sometimes lead to a model destabilization[9]:

- the evolution of political coalitions of interest and priorities gradually leading to a shift in the institutional hierarchy or changes in institutional complementarity;
- long-term structural changes that affect capitalism and its dynamics (growth regime): globalization, population ageing, technological change, development of the service sector, climate change, etc.
- the permanent interaction between institutions and organizations/firms in an open economy, which leads to an incremental change in the rules of the game (North, 1990).

Hence, it is difficult not to recognize that the French or Swedish models have evolved considerably since the 1980s. However, elements of their institutional complementarity remain.

Application to Central and Eastern European Countries

The post-socialist transformation of the 1990s and 2000s provides a unique opportunity for the comparative analysis of models of capitalism. First, the question of the outcome of the transition arises. What models of capitalism are likely to emerge from this process of systemic change? Will

[9] Boyer (2005b, 2015) refers to «endometabolism», the development of tensions within an institutional architecture, a victim of its own success, and «hybridization», the assimilation of imported institutions into a given configuration.

the CEECs represent a new family of path-dependent capitalisms after the transition? Or will they individually join the different types of European capitalism already identified and presented above (e.g. according to the different approaches, LME or Mediterranean capitalism)? In a second stage, the integration process is reviving the debate on the diversity of capitalism by extending it to the whole EU. Indeed, US economic performances during the 1990s, in the context of the liberal globalization, prompted governments, under pressure from international organizations, to adopt the same kind of institutions as the Anglo-Saxon model. This is also the meaning of the message addressed by the EU to candidate countries, following in this respect the EBRD and Washington Consensus (Williamson, 1990) recommendations of the early 1990s. The outbreak of the financial crisis in 2008 contributed to slowing this process but did not stop it.

A lot of research focused on the CEECs can be classified on the basis of their proximity to the two major approaches discussed earlier, the *régulationist* one (Boyer, 1995; Berrou & Carrincazeaux, 2005; Chavance & Magnin, 2000, 2002; Farkas, 2011, 2016; Magnin, 1999; McMenamin, 2004; Mykhnenko, 2007a, 2007b) and the VoC (Adam et al., 2009; Ban, 2013; Buchen, 2007; Egan & Neumann, 1999; Feldmann, 2006; King, 2007; Nölke & Vliegenthart, 2009). Yet, some authors have developed their own typologies, arguing that both approaches are not suitable for transition countries (Bohle & Greskovits, 2007, 2012; Cernat, 2006; Drahokoupil & Myant, 2011; Lane, 2005; Mihalyi & Szelenyi, 2020; Myant, 2007) (see Table 2.1).

LME, CME or DME in Central and Eastern Europe?

A first set of studies, using the VoC typology, have focused on Estonia and Slovenia, arguing they are respectively good examples of liberal and coordinated market economies. Feldmann (2006) puts the emphasis on industrial relations as a central component of the VoC framework and provides less detailed analysis of the other activity spheres. He shows that the Slovenian model «represents a consensual and coordinated approach to industrial relations and social dialogue, with strong employers' organizations and unions, and also exceptionally high coverage of collective agreements» (Feldman, 2006, p. 841). By contrast, the Estonian industrial relations system exhibits all the characteristics of LMEs with decentralized wage negotiations, limited coverage of collective agreements and

Table 2.1 Varieties of capitalism in CEECs and varieties of typology

Authors	*Emerging models*	*Countries*	*Theoretical framework*
Egan and Neumann (1999)	• Hybrid model between Anglo-Saxon capitalism and Rhenish model	• Czech Republic	Albert (1993)
Magnin (1999)	• Post-socialist emergent capitalism	• Baltic States, Croatia, Czech Republic, Hungary, Poland, Slovakia, Slovenia	*Régulation* theory
McMenamin (2004)	• Original model of East-Central European capitalist democracy tending towards Mediterranean capitalism	• Czech Republic, Hungary, Poland	VoC, Esping-Andersen (1990) and Lijphart (1999)
Berrou and Carrincazeaux (2005)	• East-Central European capitalism, close to Mediterranean capitalism	• Czech Republic, Hungary, Poland	*Régulation* theory
Lane (2005)	• Continental capitalism • Hybrid capitalism state/market • Non-capitalist model	• New EU member states • Russia, Ukraine, Kazakhstan, Georgia, Moldova • Uzbekistan, Belarus, Turkmenistan	VoC, *Régulation* theory, Coates (2000)
• Cernat (2006) • Myant (2007)	• Cocktail capitalism • "Combined" capitalism	• Romania • Czech Republic	• Specific approach + Rhodes and van Apeldoorn (1997) • Neither VoC nor *Régulation* but a combination of different models
Buchen (2007) Feldmann (2006)	• LME • CME	• Estonia • Slovenia	VoC

(continued)

Table 2.1 (continued)

Authors	*Emerging models*	*Countries*	*Theoretical framework*
King (2007)	• Liberal dependent capitalism • Patrimonial post-communist capitalism	• Czech Republic, Hungary, Poland • Russia, Ukraine, Romania	VoC
Mykhnenko (2007a, 2007b)	• Mixed market economies (MME) or Mediterranean capitalism	• Poland, Ukraine	VoC and *Régulation* theory
Bohle and Greskovits (2007, 2012)	• Neoliberal capitalism • Embedded neoliberal capitalism • Neocorporatism	• Baltic states • Czech Republic, Hungary, Poland, Slovakia • Slovenia	Specific approach (Polanyi)
Drahokoupil (2007)	• Porterian workfare postnational regime	• Czech Republic, Hungary, Poland, Slovakia	*Régulation* theory
Crowley (2008)	• CME • LME	• Slovenia • All other new EU member states	VoC
Nölke and Vliegenthart (2009)	• Dependent market economies (DME)	• Czech Republic, Hungary, Poland, Slovakia	VoC
Adam et al. (2009)	• Managerial capitalism • Liberal (market) capitalism	• Slovenia • Estonia	VoC, *Régulation* theory, Schmidt (2002)

Authors	*Emerging models*	*Countries*	*Theoretical framework*
Magnin (2009)	• Continental capitalism • Mediterranean capitalism • Anglo-Saxon capitalism	• Czech Republic, Hungary, Slovenia • Romania, Poland • Baltic states, Slovakia	*Régulation* theory
Drahokoupil and Myant (2011)	• FDI-based market economies • Peripheral market economies • Oligarchic or clientelistic capitalism • Order states • Remittance- and aid-based economies	• Czech Republic, Hungary, Poland, Slovakia • Baltic states, Southeastern Europe • Russia and some CIS countries • Belarus, Uzbekistan •Albania, Moldova, Armenia	Specific approach
Farkas (2011, 2016)	• Original model of "Central and Eastern European capitalism"	• New EU member states	*Régulation* theory
Ban (2013)	• Dependent market economies (DME)	• Romania	VoC
Mihalyi and Szelenyi (2020)	• Liberal capitalism • Illiberal capitalism	• New EU member states except below • Hungary (since 2010), Poland (since 2015), Russia...	Specific approach (even if references to VoC)

Source own elaboration

weakness of both unions and employers' organizations. Crowley (2008) also focuses on industrial relations. He concludes that Slovenia is very close to the CME ideal-type but that all of the other new EU member states look much more like LMEs.

Buchen (2007) confirms Feldmann's results and extends his analysis of industrial relations to the other activity spheres at the core of the VoC theory and to the dynamics of comparative institutional advantages. He shows that both countries exhibit a high degree of complementary institutions. In Slovenia, the industrial relations system is complementary to a highly protected labour market, while the vocational training system provides specific skills. In Estonia, industrial relations and labour market features are complementary to a vocational training system reshaped towards general education. Trade figures and patterns of foreign direct investment complete the picture and reveal comparative institutional advantages of CME type in Slovenia and LME type in Estonia. As the VoC approach predicts, different clusters of complementary institutions may result in equally good macroeconomic performances. This has been the case for Slovenia and Estonia during the transition process.[10]

Another interesting example of applying the VoC framework to post-socialist countries is Nölke and Vliegenthart (2009)'s work on the «dependent» type of capitalism.[11] Their approach is different from that of the preceding authors as they try to broaden the original VoC binary typology. They actually assume that a third variety of capitalism is emerging in Central-Eastern Europe (the Czech Republic, Hungary, Poland, Slovakia), the dependent market economy (DME), which should not be confused with CME or LME. The salient feature of the DME variety is the fundamental dependence on foreign capital.

Régulationist and Cluster Analysis

Among the *régulationist*-oriented studies devoted to the CEECs, based on Amable's statistical methodology, we could mention first of all Berrou

[10] Adam et al. (2009) also studied the Slovenian and Estonian cases. They are rather critical about the existing typologies, such as the VoC or Amable's work. Yet, their conclusions are not so far from the VoC paradigm since they oppose the Slovenian managerial capitalism with a corporatist welfare state to the Estonian liberal (market) capitalism.

[11] The issue of dependence and dependent capitalism will be developed in the next chapter.

and Carrincazeaux (2005). Resting on the Czech, Hungarian and Polish cases, they show the existence of a sixth homogeneous group of capitalist countries in Central Europe at the beginning of the 2000s. Still, they are not convinced it can be considered as a real new and stable model of capitalism because the countries under study are still at a transitional stage. Hence, it is difficult to assess the stability of complementarity relations between institutions. Is this group of countries eventually evolving towards an existing model of capitalism? According to the authors, it shares some common features with the Mediterranean model of capitalism as far as the financial sector, the welfare state or education are concerned, but could also tend towards the market-based capitalism because of the spread of liberalization reforms in Europe. Hungary is notably ahead on the road to the Anglo-Saxon model as far as the product and labour markets are concerned.

Mykhnenko's work (2007a, 2007b) is focused on two countries, Poland and Ukraine, between the mid-1990s and mid-2000s. Both countries share some institutional characteristics which are designing an original model of «post-communist capitalism» but, as Berrou and Carrincazeaux have already noticed, which is still «at a formative stage». Their financial system is notably underdeveloped compared to Western European economies. In his 2007b article, the author refers to Poland and Ukraine as hybrid forms, «mixed or weakly coordinated market economies» (MMEs), which differ from both liberal market economies (LME) and coordinated market economies (CME). Mykhnenko concludes that the post-communist emerging model in Poland and Ukraine presents a certain degree of institutional complementarity which could (partially) explain the positive socio-economic developments experienced by both countries in the early 2000s.[12]

In her 2016 book, Farkas builds on earlier work (Farkas, 2011) to characterize, on the basis of Amable's statistical method, the economic model emerging in the new EU Member States (except Croatia) in the 2000s. She confirms that these countries represent a specific family of capitalisms, which she calls, for want of a better term, the «Central and Eastern European model», whose characteristics set it apart from other Western

[12] The reference to the VoC categories here seems rather surprising since Amable's methodological and theoretical framework is widely used in the paper. It is a good example of the usual confusion between both theoretical approaches. Nevertheless, we consider Mykhnenko's papers should be classified within the *régulationist* school.

European families. Even if for certain «institutional domains» identified by Amable (education system), they are closer to the continental model, for others (wage-labour nexus, social welfare) they are closer to the Anglo-Saxon model. For the author, the Central and Eastern European capitalism is the path-dependent outcome of post-socialist transformation trajectories. According to her, the shortage of capital and management skills, a weak civil society and the influence of international organizations and the EU on structural reforms are the main initial conditions behind that outcome. Therefore, this new model of capitalism cannot be considered as a transient configuration but rather as a permanent one, all the more so as it shows an evident complementarity between its founding institutions. The author acknowledges a relative dependence on FDI and a possibility of being locked into a lesser path of development because of the fundamental asymmetrical position between the old Europe and its periphery in the international division of labour.

Looking for Specific Approaches

Finally, some researchers have preferred to develop their own typologies, assessing that both previous approaches (VoC and *Régulation*) were not suited to CEECs reality, given the legacy of the former socialist system.

Drahokoupil and Myant (2011) consider that the VoC «paradigm» or Amable's theory is not adequate to analyse the diversity of capitalism among transition economies. Specific features of transition economies make these approaches, built to explain Western capitalism, useless to analyse post-socialist reality. Some well-established institutions in advanced economies are not so developed in former socialist economies, such as state capacity, the rule of law, corporate governance, the financial system, the separation between business and politics, and so on. Moreover, long-term continuity and stability are underlying hypotheses in the VoC framework, whereas continual changes have characterized transition economies. Under these conditions, Drahokoupil and Myant prefer to build their own approach by focusing first on the form of international integration, considered as the main problem in post-socialist countries. Each country presents a mix of different forms of integration. And by combining forms of integration and key institutional features such as the nature of property rights, the role of the state and the nature of the relation between the state and main economic actors, five types of post-socialist capitalism can be distinguished. The first one is *FDI-based market economies*, typical of Central-Eastern European countries. They are characterized by democratic political systems, a form of international integration based on the export of high-value products into Western Europe, generally manufactured inside branches of large multinational companies. EU integration helps develop state capacity and secure the legal and business environment. The welfare state is relatively developed to sustain social peace. *Peripheral market economies* represent the second type of capitalism. South-Eastern European countries and the Baltic states belong to this category characterized by democratic political systems and good conditions for business but with a less complex structure of exports. This model is often associated with a residual welfare state. *Oligarchic or clientelistic capitalism* is often found in the CIS. Russia is a case in point. The political system is generally more authoritarian and the relation between business and politics is closer than in the previous models of capitalism. The level of foreign investment is generally low and the dependence on raw material exports inherent to this model. The commodity rent is concentrated in the hands of the economic and political oligarchy. *Order states* is the fourth model, typical of CIS countries with limited reforms. They are characterized by authoritarian regimes. International integration depends on state support for export. The welfare state remains generous so as to buy the support of the population. Finally, *remittance- and aid-based economies* are typical of low-income countries in the CIS and Eastern Europe.

Bohle and Greskovits (2012) reject the VoC approach, created to explain Western developed economies but ill-suited for analysing post-socialist economies. Therefore, they prefer to build their own theoretical and comparative framework resting on Polanyi's work. They put the emphasis on political factors. The (perceived) legacy of the former socialist system, the impact of radical uncertainty and crises on structural reforms and the major influence of transnational actors have all contributed to shape East European capitalisms. Their book is focused on institutional change in the new EU member states between 1990 and 2010. They show the emergence of three new varieties of capitalism in Central and Eastern Europe: the *pure neoliberal* type in the Baltic states, the *embedded neoliberal* capitalism in the Visegrád countries and the *neocorporatist* model in Slovenia. In the Baltic countries, the emergence of the *neoliberal* capitalism is the outcome of a radical reform strategy related to the issue of nation-state building and the negative perception of Soviet legacy. The radical transformation strategy appears to be the best way to break with the past. And national independence is the highest priority. To protect citizens from the economic and social costs of transformation is therefore not at the top of the agenda. Estonia has implemented the most comprehensive strategy and played the leading role in the region, followed by Latvia and then Lithuania. Baltic governments were the first to implement a flat tax regime and a three-pillar pension system. Despite negative social consequences, the neoliberal model has remained unchallenged. In Central Europe, the *embedded neoliberal* capitalism is an unexpected outcome of the post-socialist transformation process. Initially, politicians showed rather a preference for a "national" capitalism based on the development of a middle class of domestic owners. The Visegrád countries succeeded instead in maintaining a relatively generous welfare state, a legacy of the former socialist period, and in strengthening social cohesion, while pursuing the conflictual objectives of liberalizing their economies and competing to attract foreign direct investments. Huge inflows of foreign capital have resulted in an impressive industrial development driven by export-oriented transnational companies. In Southeastern Europe, only Slovenia turned into a performing labour-inclusive *neocorporatist* model. In Bulgaria, Romania and Croatia, state weakness highly constrained national transformation trajectories and contributed to deep crises in the mid-1990s. EU accession considerably helped these countries to escape from their buoyant earlier paths. In the mid-2000s, after a decade of accelerated liberal reforms, Bulgaria and Romania seem to move closer to the Baltic neoliberal model and Croatia to the embedded neoliberal capitalism.

Conclusion

Since the 1990s, we have observed an increasing number of publications in the field of comparative capitalism. Central and Eastern Europe has provided a fertile ground for the development of this research. Various typologies have emerged, notably approaches in terms of varieties or diversity of capitalism. In our view, they should not be confused as they are based on very different theoretical frameworks. In this respect, the theoretical framework of the *Régulation* school is the most accomplished—but not the most influential in the debates—because it is a full-fledged theory on the dynamics of capitalism, which encompasses the question of the diversity of national trajectories in time and space (Boyer, 2015). Nevertheless, RT may be criticized for a theoretical construct based on the institutional configurations of Western economies and may thus seem ill-suited to ex-socialist economies in transition or to developing economies (Magnin et al., 2018). Two observations are worth mentioning here.

First, authors criticizing RT are not so far from it eventually. Bohle and Greskovits (2012) or Drahokoupil and Myant (2011) both criticize the VoC or RT paradigm. However, their criticisms should be qualified by the following remarks. First, Bohle and Greskovits tend to ignore the other, *régulationist*, theoretical framework, which seems rather relevant to understand their analysis. Moreover, international integration modalities, one of the key institutional domains of the *Régulation* theory, play a major role in their approach. Second, isn't the neoliberal type of capitalism a Baltic version of the Anglo-Saxon model? Aren't the embedded neoliberal and the neocorporatist capitalisms very similar to the European continental and the social-democratic models, respectively, we all find in Amable's approach? Drahokoupil and Myant, for their part, do not ignore the régulationist framework but, as aforementioned, they consider it as ill-suited for post-socialist countries. However, they also put the emphasis on international integration and on the role of the state, which sound also quite *régulationist*.[13]

Second, a number of authors admit the decisive role of FDI in the emergent capitalism in Central and Eastern Europe. The 2008 crisis brought to light the vulnerabilities inherent to this «dependent» capitalism. Furthermore, dependency theories seem to be a way to remedy the Western bias of *Régulation* theory.

References

Adam, F., Kristan, P., & Tomsic, M. (2009). Varieties of capitalism in Eastern Europe (with special emphasis on Estonia and Slovenia). *Communist and Post-Communist Studies, 42*, 65–81.

Aiginger, K. (2005). Towards a new European model of a reformed welfare state: An alternative to the United States model. In *Economic survey of Europe* (pp. 105–114). United Nations.

Albert, M. (1993). *Capitalism against capitalism*. Whurr Publishers.

[13] In a 2007 article, Drahokoupil defined the economic model in the Visegrád countries as a «Porterian workfare postnational regime» (Table 2.1). He himself recognized the *régulationist* influence in this approach.

Amable, B. (2000). Institutional complementarity and diversity of social systems of innovation and production. *Review of International Political Economy, 7*(4), 645–687.

Amable, B. (2003). *The diversity of modern capitalism.* Oxford University Press.

Amable, B. (2009). Structural reforms in Europe and the (in)coherence of institutions. *Oxford Review of Economic Policy, 25*(1), 17–39.

Amable, B., Barré, R., & Boyer, R. (1997). *Les systèmes d'innovation à l'ère de la globalisation.* Economica.

Amable, B., & Palombarini, S. (2008). A neorealist approach to institutional change and the diversity of capitalism. *Socio-Economic Review, 7*, 123–143.

Aoki, M. (1994). The contingent governance of teams: Analysis of institutional complementarity. *International Economic Review, 35*(3), 657–676.

Ban, C. (2013). *From cocktail to dependence: Revisiting the foundations of dependent market economies* (GEGI Working Paper No. 3).

Becker, U., & Vasileva, A. (2017). Russia's political economy re-conceptualised: A changing hybrid of liberalism, statism and patrimonialism. *Journal of Eurasian Studies, 8*(1), 83–96.

Berrou, J.-P., & Carrincazeaux, C. (2005, September). La diversité des capitalismes et les pays d'Europe centrale et orientale: une analyse statistique. *Cahiers du GRES*, n°2005–18.

Bohle, D., & Greskovits, B. (2007). Neoliberalism, embedded neoliberalism and neocorporatism: Towards transnational capitalism in central-Eastern Europe. *West European Politics, 30*(3), 443–466.

Bohle, D., & Greskovits, B. (2012). *Capitalist diversity on Europe's periphery.* Cornell University Press.

Boyer, R. (1990). *The regulation school: A critical introduction.* Columbia University Press.

Boyer, R. (1995). The great transformation of Eastern Europe: A "regulationist" perspective. *Emergo Journal of Transforming Economies and Societies, 2*(4), 25–41.

Boyer, R. (1996, October). *The seven paradoxes of capitalism…or is a theory of modern economies still possible?* (Cepremap Working Paper No. 9620).

Boyer, R. (2000). Is a finance-led growth regime a viable alternative to Fordism? A preliminary analysis. *Economy and Society, 29*(1), 111–145.

Boyer, R. (2005a). How and why capitalisms differ. *Economy and Society, 34*(4), 509–557.

Boyer, R. (2005b). Coherence, diversity and the evolution of capitalisms: The institutional complementarity hypothesis. *Evolutionary and Institutional Economic Review, 2*(1), 43–80.

Boyer, R. (2011). *Les financiers détruiront-ils le capitalisme?* Economica.

Boyer, R. (2015). *Économie politique des capitalismes. Théorie de la régulation et des crises.* La Découverte.

Buchen, C. (2007). Estonia and Slovenia as antipodes. In D. Lane & M. Myant (Eds.), *Varieties of capitalism in postcommunist countries* (pp. 65–89). Palgrave Macmillan.

Cernat, L. (2006). *Europeanization, varieties of capitalism and economic performance in Central and Eastern Europe*. Palgrave Macmillan.

Chavance, B. (2008). *Institutional economics*. Routledge.

Chavance, B. (2019). *The transformation of communist systems: Economic reform since the 1950s*. Routledge.

Chavance, B., & Magnin, E. (2000). National trajectories of post-socialist transformation: Is there a convergence towards western capitalisms? In M. Dobry (Ed.), *Democratic and capitalist transitions in Eastern Europe: Lessons for the social sciences* (pp. 221–233). Kluwer Academic Publishers.

Chavance, B., & Magnin, E. (2002). Emergence of path-dependent mixed economies in Central Europe. In G. Hodgson (Ed.), *A modern reader in institutional and evolutionary economics: Key concepts* (pp. 168–200). Edward Elgar.

Coates, D. (2000). *Models of capitalism: Growth and stagnation in the modern era*. Polity Press.

Crowley, S. (2008, April). *Does labor still matter? East European labor and varieties of capitalism* (NCEEER Report).

Drahokoupil, J. (2007). The state of the capitalist state in East-Central Europe: Towards the porterian workfare post-national regime. In B. Sergi, W. Bagatelas, & J. Kubicova (Eds.), *Industries and markets in Central and Eastern Europe*. Ashgate.

Drahokoupil, J., & Myant, M. (2011). *Transition economies: Political economy in Russia, Eastern Europe, and Central Asia*. Wiley.

Ebenau, M. (2012). Varieties of capitalism or dependency? A critique of the VoC approach for Latin America. *Competition and Change, 16*(3), 206–223.

Egan, M., & Neumann, S. (1999). Between German and Anglo-Saxon capitalism: The Czech financial markets in transition. *New Political Economy, 4*(3), 173–194.

Esping-Andersen, G. (1990). *The three worlds of welfare capitalism*. Polity Press.

Farkas, B. (2011). The Central and Eastern European model of capitalism. *Post-Communist Economies, 23*(1), 15–34.

Farkas, B. (2016). *Models of capitalism in the European Union*. Palgrave Macmillan.

Feldmann, M. (2006). Emerging varieties of capitalism in transition countries. Industrial relations and wage bargaining in Estonia and Slovenia. *Comparative Political Studies, 39*(7), 829–854.

Feldmann, M. (2019). Global varieties of capitalism. *World politics, 71*(1), 162–196.

Hall, P., & Soskice, D. (Eds.). (2001). *Varieties of capitalism: The institutional foundations of comparative advantage*. Oxford University Press.

Hodgson, G. (1993). *Economics and evolution: Bringing life back into economics*. Polity Press.

King, L. (2007). Central European capitalism in comparative perspective. In B. Hancké, M. Rhodes, & M. Thatcher (Eds.), *Beyond varieties of capitalism. conflict, contradictions and complementarities in the European economy* (pp. 307–327). Oxford University Press.

Kornai, J. (1980). *Economics of shortage (vol. A and B)*. North Holland Publishing Company.

Lane, D. (2005). Emerging varieties of capitalism in former state socialist societies. *Competition and Change, 9*(3), 227–247.

Lijphart, A. (1999). *Patterns of democracy: Government forms and performance in thirty-six countries*. Yale University Press.

Magnin, E. (1999). La contribution des économies post-socialistes à la diversité du capitalisme. In B. Chavance, E. Magnin, R. Motamed-Nejad, & J. Sapir (Eds), *Capitalisme et socialisme en perspective. Évolution et transformations des systèmes économiques* (pp. 349–370). La Découverte.

Magnin, E. (2002). Path-dependence and initial conditions in the transition process: The cases of Hungary and Romania. *East-West Journal of Economics and Business, 5*(1), 67–87.

Magnin, E. (2009). Concurrence fiscale et modèle social dans l'Europe élargie: Convergence ou désunion européenne? *Revue D'études Comparatives Est-Ouest, 40*(2), 55–86.

Magnin, E., Delteil, V., & Vercueil, J. (2018). La dépendance dans les relations entre capitalismes nationaux: quelle portée analytique? *Revue de la Régulation* [on line], 24, 2nd semester/Autumn.

May, C., & Nölke, A. (2018). Dangers of residual dependency in state-permeated capitalism: The case of Brazil during labor party rule. *Revue de la Régulation, 24*(2), 1–24.

McMenamin, I. (2004). Varieties of capitalist democracy: What difference does East-Central Europe make? *Journal of Public Policy, 24*(3), 259–274.

Meyer, M., Milgrom, P., & Roberts, J. (1992). Organizational prospects, influence costs, and ownership changes. *Journal of Economics and Management Strategy, 1*, 9–35.

Mihalyi, P., & Szelenyi, I. (2020). The two forms of modern capitalism: Liberal and illiberal states. A criticism of the varieties of capitalism paradigm. *Comparative Sociology, 19*, 155–175.

Myant, M. (2007). The Czech Republic: From 'Czech' capitalism to 'European' capitalism. In D. Lane & M. Myant (Eds.), *Varieties of capitalism in post-communist countries* (pp. 13–39). Palgrave Macmillan.

Mykhnenko, V. (2007a). Poland and Ukraine: Institutional structures and economic performance. In D. Lane & M. Myant (Eds.), *Varieties of capitalism in post-communist countries* (pp. 124–145). Palgrave Macmillan.

Mykhnenko, V. (2007b). Strengths and weaknesses of 'weak' coordination: Economic institutions, revealed comparative advantages, and socio-economic performance of mixed market economies in Poland and Ukraine. In B. Hancké, M. Rhodes, & M. Thatcher (Eds.), *Beyond varieties of capitalism: Conflict, contradictions and complementarities in the European economy* (pp. 351–378). Oxford University Press.

Nölke, A., & Vliegenthart, A. (2009). Enlarging the variety of capitalism. The emergence of dependent market economies in East Central Europe. *World Politics, 61*(4), 670–702.

North, D. (1990). *Institutions, institutional change and economic performance.* Cambridge University Press.

Petit, P. (2005). *Croissance et richesse des nations* (Repères n°419). La Découverte.

Rhodes, M., & Van Apeldoorn, B. (1997). Capitalism versus capitalism in Western Europe. In M. Rhodes, P., Heywood, V., & Wright (Eds.), *Developments in Western European politics.* St. Martins Press.

Sapir, A. (2005, November). Globalization and the reform of European social models. *Bruegel Policy Brief.*

Schedelik, M., Nölke, A., Mertens, D., & May, C. (2021). Comparative capitalism, growth models and emerging markets: The development of the field. *New Political Economy, 26*(4), 514–526.

Schlumberger, O. (2008). Structural reform, economic order, and development: Patrimonial capitalism. *Review of International Political Economy, 15*(4), 622–649.

Schmidt, V. (2002). *The futures of European capitalism.* Oxford University Press.

Schneider, B. R. (2009). Hierarchical market economies and varieties of capitalism in Latin America. *Journal of Latin American Studies, 41*(3), 553–575.

Vasileva-Dienes, A., & Schmidt, V. A. (2019). Conceptualising capitalism in the twenty-first century: The BRICS and the European periphery. *Contemporary Politics, 25*(3), 255–275.

Williamson, J. (1990). What Washington means by policy reform. In J. Williamson (Ed.), *Latin American adjustment: How much has happened?* (Chapter 2). Institute for International Economics.

CHAPTER 3

Dependent Capitalism

Abstract For some authors presented in the previous chapter, the post-socialist transformation has led to the emergence of a form of dependent capitalism. This hypothesis gained in relevance during the 2000s. The purpose of this chapter is to present the model of dependent capitalism. The concept of dependence initially refers to the 1960s and 1970s research on Latin America within a Marxist theoretical framework. It is then used to designate «peripheral» economies whose growth depends on the decisions of actors belonging to the hegemonic «centre». However, it reappears today to qualify CEE economies in a theoretical and historical context that is very different from that of this original filiation. From a theoretical point of view, it can be considered at first glance as an extension of the VoC approach applied to the CEECs. Moreover, the 2008 financial crisis acted as a revelation of CEECs' vulnerabilities, related to outward-oriented growth models, and reinforced the relevance of an analysis in terms of dependent capitalism.

Keywords Dependent capitalism · Dependency theories · Dependent development · Imperialism · Foreign direct investment · Dependent market economies (DMEs) · (2008) Financial crisis

E. Magnin and N. Nenovsky, *Diversity of Capitalism in Central and Eastern Europe*, https://doi.org/10.1007/978-3-031-04950-7_3

For some authors presented in the previous chapter, the post-socialist transformation process has led to the emergence of a form of dependent capitalism. This hypothesis gained in relevance during the 2000s. The concept of dependence initially refers to the 1960s and 1970s research on Latin America within a Marxist theoretical framework. Dependency theories have helped to revisit development analysis based on the theories of imperialism, although both approaches should not be confused. They are also focused on conflict/cooperation relationships between domestic and foreign actors. Dependence is typical of peripheral economies whose growth depends on the decisions of actors belonging to the hegemonic «Centre». However, the concept is reappearing today to qualify CEE economies in a theoretical and historical context that is very different from that of this original filiation. From a theoretical point of view, it falls within the scope of comparative capitalism, starting from the VoC but without dwelling on it. Regarding the historical context, it is characterized by the 2008 financial crisis, which has been revealing the vulnerabilities of CEE countries, marked by outward-oriented growth models, and reinforced the relevance of an analysis in terms of dependent capitalism.

Dependency Theories

Broadly speaking, dependency theories gather a collection of contributions, generally focused on Latin America, which were developing after World War II, emanating from social scientists, economists (Raul Prebisch, Celso Furtado, André Gunder Frank, Osvaldo Sunkel, Teothonio Dos Santos, Luiz Carlos Bresser-Pereira), but also historians (Caio Prado Jr, Sergio Bagu) or sociologists (Florestan Fernandes, Fernando Henrique Cardoso, Enzo Faletto), to name but a few, to which we can also add Samir Amin. They have contributed to renewing development and underdevelopment analysis by relying on the theories of imperialism, although they do not necessarily identify with them.

Theories of Imperialism

The classical theories of imperialism emerged at the beginning of the twentieth century with the seminal works of Hobson (1902), Rosa Luxemburg (1913) and Lenin (1917). The term imperialism does not appear in Marx's writings, even though the latter laid the foundations for a theory of the world economy that would later be elaborated. Initially, the main point was to question the evolution and functioning of the capitalist system at a particular moment in its history rather than the relationships between developed and underdeveloped countries.

According to Lenin (1917, 91), «imperialism is the monopoly stage of capitalism». This achievement is the product of history. Capitalism only became imperialism at a certain stage of its development. This evolution is the consequence of a process of concentration of production in increasingly larger companies. In doing so, free competition gave way to monopolies and thus to imperialism. Lenin states that it is possible to date precisely for Europe the advent of this «new capitalism» at the beginning of the twentieth century, after the 1900–1903 crisis. In the process, the banks also became concentrated and monopolized. They invest a large part of their capital in industry. «Money capital» is thus transformed into «industrial capital». Their mutual penetration leads to the emergence of «financial capital» and to the domination of a financial oligarchy.[1] Imperialism, the «highest stage of capitalism», corresponds to this domination of finance capital. But what is new in this new stage of capitalism is the export of capital, not just the export of goods. Surplus capital in the developed capitalist countries reduces opportunities for profitable investment. The export of capital, especially in the underdeveloped countries, increases profits, because profitability prospects are high there since wages are low, as are the prices of land and raw materials.[2] For Lenin, this movement contributed to the development of host countries for foreign capital, in which «elementary conditions for industrial development have been created, etc.» (idem, 71).

Under these conditions, colonization appears as a consequence of the domination of the large monopolist groups in this new stage of capitalism, that of finance capital, which in turn reinforces monopolies' power. «Colonial possession alone gives the monopolies complete guarantee against all contingencies in the struggle against competitors [...].

[1] Lenin refers to the work «of the Austrian Marxist Rudolf Hilferding» (1910 [1981]) on finance capital, of which he mentions, on the first page of his book, the translation into Russian of 1912.

[2] According to Rosa Luxemburg (1913), European imperialism is motivated by the incessant search for outlets related to the necessity for capitalism to seek the realization of unconsumed surplus value abroad.

The more capitalism is developed, the more strongly the shortage of raw materials is felt, the more intense the competition and the hunt for sources of raw materials throughout the whole world, the more desperate the struggle for the acquisition of colonies» (idem, 87). Once economic, the struggle becomes political. The political control of underdeveloped countries and the division of the world among great powers appear inevitable and linked to the development of capitalism. But interstate struggles for sharing the world increase the system's instability and the risk of wars. Lenin does not hesitate to rely on Hobson's work (1902) on imperialism, although he was not a Marxist, especially on the measure of the colonized territories by developed countries and on the «economic parasitism of imperialism». For Hobson, imperialism is not a good policy for Britain and benefits only a few. «Although the new Imperialism has been bad business for the nation, it has been good business for certain classes and certain trades within the nation. The vast expenditures on armaments, the costly wars, the grave risks and embarrassments of foreign policy, the stoppage of political and social reforms within Great Britain, though fraught with great injury to the nation, have served well the present business interests of certain industries and professions» (Hobson, 1902, 51–52).

Finally, Lenin considers that imperialism is defined by the following five characteristics, which summarize his thought process:

«(1) the concentration of production and capital has developed to such a high stage that it has created monopolies which play a decisive role in economic life; (2) the merging of bank capital with industrial capital, and the creation, on the basis of this "finance capital", of a financial oligarchy; (3) the export of capital as distinguished from the export of commodities acquires exceptional importance; (4) the formation of international monopolist capitalist associations which share the world among themselves, and (5) the territorial division of the whole world among the biggest capitalist powers is completed» (Lenin, 1917, 92).

Neither Lenin nor Hobson were actually interested in the consequences of imperialism for the dominated countries. It was not until the 1950s and Paul Baran's work that this type of analysis emerged. For Baran (1957), the consequences of imperialism are particularly negative for peripheral countries. In this respect, India's example is striking. A prosperous and advanced nation before British colonization, it has since regressed. According to the Marxist economist, «it was caused by the elaborate, ruthless, systematic despoliation of India by British capital from the very onset of British rule» (Baran, 1957, 278). Thus is revealed «the main task of imperialism in our time: to prevent, or, if that is impossible, to slow down and to control the economic development of underdeveloped countries. [...] For whichever aspect of economic development we may consider, it is manifestly detrimental to the prosperity of the raw-materials-producing corporations» (idem, 340). Yet Baran acknowledges that the centre countries are building infrastructures in the colonized countries (railways, ports, roads, airports, power plants, communication networks, etc.), which should a priori have a positive effect on their development. However, «their effect would still remain nil (or negative) as long as they constitute alien bodies in a socio-economic structure into which they have been artificially injected» (ibid.: 336). In order to slow down the transformation of merchant capitalism in colonized countries into industrial capitalism, multinational firms may rely on a political alliance with some local social classes that are also in favour of maintaining a status quo: merchants in business with foreign firms constituting a comprador class, local industrialists in a monopoly position and feudal landowners. «What results is a political and social coalition of wealthy compradors, powerful monopolists, and large landowners dedicated to the defence of the existing feudal-mercantile order. [...] - this coalition has nothing to hope for from the rise of industrial capitalism which would dislodge it from its positions of privilege and power» (ibid., 338). If necessary, multinational firms can receive protection and military support from their country of origin, especially in colonized countries. Benefiting from a monopoly situation in peripheral countries, foreign companies have no interest in taking risks and investing in their development and prefer to repatriate most profits. We find the same triad, present in Lenin and Hobson, imperialism-monopoly-colonization. This results in long-lasting economic stagnation and underdevelopment in the periphery.

From Imperialism to Dependency

In addressing the consequences of imperialism for the dominated countries, Baran announces dependency theories because «the word dependence applied to the periphery is the counterpart of the word imperialism applied to the center» (Bresser-Pereira, 2009, 538), even if both should not be confused. However, the 1960s increase in FDI and industrial production in peripheral countries, especially in Latin America, seems to challenge Baran's argument, pointing to the possibility of both imperialism and a form of development in the periphery, which dependency theories will try to explain (Evans, 1979).

Dos Santos' (1970, 231) definition of dependence is generally accepted. It is «a situation in which the economy of certain countries is conditioned by the development and expansion of another economy to which the former is subjected». Growth and capital accumulation depend on economic decisions made by actors outside the country. As Evans (1979, 27) points out, «dependence is then defined most simply as a situation in which the rate and direction of accumulation are externally conditioned».

Frank's (1967) studies on Latin America are generally considered as seminal for Marxist dependency theories because Frank was an eminent Marxist economist. However, Cardoso (1977) thinks that this established authorship does not do justice to the many South American scholars (Bagu, Caio Prado, Furtado, Fernandes, etc.) who contributed to new analyses on the colonial period and feudalism in Latin America—before Frank. Nevertheless, the latter remains the source of the distinction between metropolitan centres and peripheral satellites.

The main difference with the theories of imperialism, apart from the change of perspective on the side of the dominated countries, is the emphasis on social class relations within dependent capitalism. Imperialism primarily focused on exploitation by the centre as an explanation for underdevelopment. The dependency approach does not reject imperialism, which is associated with the global expansion of capitalism and foreign capital inflows, but it refuses the mechanical opposition between external and internal actors and favours an analysis involving the contradictory historical dynamics (alliances and conflicts) between foreign interests and some local social classes. «What was significant was «the movement», the class struggles, the redefinitions of interest, the political alliances that maintained the structures while at the same time opening the possibility of their transformation» (Cardoso, 1977, 14).

Among dependency theories, two approaches are generally distinguished (Bresser-Pereira, 2009; Cardoso, 1977): an approach centred on workers' overexploitation and the «dependent-associated development» model. The first one is the historical, original approach of dependency. It is associated with Frank's work (1967) and related to the theories of imperialism. For him, South American countries became capitalist following the fifteenth-century Iberian conquests under the mercantile form of capitalism. On a world scale, capitalism is structured in metropolitan centres and satellites, and this structure is repeated at different regional, national and local levels. Underdevelopment is part of this hierarchical structure. It is produced and maintained by capitalism. The metropoles suck up the economic surplus generated by satellites and hinder their development. Hence, they become more and more dominant and the satellites more and more dependent. For Frank (1967, 9), economic development and underdevelopment are two sides of the same coin. «One and the same historical process of the expansion and development of capitalism throughout the world has simultaneously generated - and continues to generate - both economic development and structural underdevelopment». Dos Santos (1970) follows the same line and argues that, whatever the historical form of dependence (colonial, financial-industrial, technological-industrial), domestic market growth is constrained by various factors, notably labour overexploitation, which limits its purchasing power, and the repatriation of profits generated in the satellite country into imperialist centres.

The second approach to dependency, the «dependent-associated development» model, is derived from the Sao Paulo school sociologists' work, Cardoso and Faletto in particular (Cardoso & Faletto, 1979). It considers that development is not incompatible with the idea of dependency, and hence, both can be associated. Multinationals and foreign capital contribute to the country's industrialization and growth. Then «dependent development implies both the accumulation of capital and some degree of industrialization on the periphery. Dependent development is a special instance of dependency, characterized by the association or alliance of international and local capital. The state also joins the alliance...» (Evans, 1979, 32). However, dependent development does not eliminate the contradictions between centre and periphery. As Cardoso (1977, 20) points out, «when one examines the relationship between the economies of 'dependent-associated development' and the central economies, it is not hard to perceive that the international division of labor persists, based on very unequal degrees of wealth, on unequal forms of appropriation of the international surplus, and on the monopolization of the dynamic capitalist sectors by the central countries. The sectors of production of capital goods and the generation of new technologies [...] remain in the central nuclei of the multinational firms...» Dependent development as well as the alliance between internal and external forces cannot be generalized to all peripheral countries. Evans refers here to the emergence of «semi-peripheral» countries theorized by Immanuel Wallerstein (1974).[3]

Dependency theorists generally identify several historical periods in Latin America corresponding to different forms of dependency evolving over time (Dos Santos, 1970; Furtado, 1965; Girvan, 1973; Sunkel, 1973). We thus find a first period of «colonial dependence», from the seventeenth century to the beginning of the nineteenth century, marked by the imperialist and monopolistic domination of colonizing countries. Primary agricultural products and precious metals are typical of colonial foreign trade. The second period, of «financial-industrial dependency» or «outward-looking development», from the second half of the nineteenth century to the Great Depression, corresponds to international trade development related to the industrial revolution in the centre countries. Associated with the urban bourgeoisie, foreign investors bring their capital in the sectors exporting raw materials and agricultural products to developed country markets. Finally, the last period of «technological-industrial dependence» or «inward-looking development» (industrialization through import substitution) developed after World War II until the 1970s. During this period, «the penetration of the multinationals becomes more intense as import substitution moves from consumer nondurables to consumer durables, intermediary goods, and some capital goods» (Evans, 1979, 30). Each period is nevertheless interpreted differently by the authors according to the different approaches to dependency presented above. For example, the last period can be considered as a phase of dependent development or continued overexploitation.

[3] Bresser-Pereira (2009) identifies a third approach to dependency, so-called «national-dependent», to which he links Sunkel, Furtado (and himself). This approach recognizes the dependence of Latin American elites on the centre countries and their consumption model, but also their desire for independence and identification with their nation. «The nationalism of development is a force of national affirmation, an aspiration to self-determination and sovereignty, a desire to participate in the benefits and creation of modern and universal culture and science, the desire to attain liberty, democracy, equality of opportunities and well-being, which the more industrialized countries enjoy to a greater or lesser extent» (Sunkel, 1969, 32).

Dependent Capitalism in Central and Eastern European Countries

The concept of dependent capitalism reappears in the 2000s in a very different theoretical and historical context to refer to Central and Eastern European economies (Magnin et al., 2018). It is moving away from the original Marxist framework and from imperialism to fall within the field of Comparative Capitalism. Still, it is a critical version of the latter, combining the VoC approach with critical international political economy emphasizing power relations, alliances and conflicts between internal and external actors and asymmetric interactions between national models of capitalism (Ebenau et al., 2015; May & Nölke, 2018). In doing so, it moves closer to the *régulationist* research agenda (Boyer, 1990) and reconnects with the sociological tradition of dependency theories, that of Cardoso and Faletto's dependent-associated development.

Dependent Market Economies

While Nölke and Vliegenthart (2009) confirm the emergence of a model of dependent capitalism in Central-Eastern Europe, it is King (2002) who first puts forward this hypothesis for Central European and Baltic countries, especially in the Polish case. King criticizes the «smithian» approach to the transition to a market economy and opts for a sociological approach that is notably based on Max Weber's and David Stark's (1992) work. However, he makes no reference to Hall and Soskice's or Boyer's work. For him, as for Stark, the outcome of the post-socialist transition is path-dependent. Alliances and conflicts among social classes inherited from the old socialist system (workers, managers, intellectuals, bureaucrats) influence the privatization process and firms' restructuring (or not), which lead at the macroeconomic level to the emergence of capitalist models with distinctive characteristics. In Russia, the alliance between former enterprise directors and bureaucracy results in the emergence of a «capitalism from above» which undermines an efficient firm restructuring and facilitates the development of clientelistic relations in a context of severe transformational recession, credit squeeze and state decline. This trajectory leads to the emergence of a «patrimonial capitalism», a crony capitalism based on raw materials export. The author considers that this model applies to the former USSR and Eastern Europe.

By contrast, in Poland, as in other Central-Eastern European and Baltic countries, the alliance of intellectuals and technocrats has led to a «capitalism from without» and a privatization process that favours foreign investors, who provide capital, technology and know-how. This process results in the emergence of a dependent capitalism «because accumulation is dependent on the import of capital and the export of manufactured products» (King, 2002, 4). «As a result, it will be vulnerable to economic shocks because of its liberalized exchange rate regime and open capital market» (idem, 26). This model of capitalism may be virtuous and lead to a convergence towards Western European living standards «if there is enough investment and technology transfer, leading to enough capture of world market share» (ibid. 26).

Following King, Nölke and Vliegenthart (2009) argue that a new variety of capitalism has been emerging in East-Central Europe (the Czech Republic, Hungary, Poland, Slovakia) since the 2000s: the "dependent market economies" (DMEs). Their theoretical framework directly derives from the VoC approach by Hall and Soskice (2001). The DME variety broadens the initial and often criticized binary typology separating the "coordinated market economies" (CMEs), with Germany as a case in point, from the "liberal market economies" (LMEs) exemplified by the United States (see Chapter 2). It also allows to take into account multinational firms' influence in the analysis.

Nölke and Vliegenthart believe that DMEs can be considered as a genuine variety of capitalism, different from both other models, because its founding institutions, as Hall and Soskice define them (industrial relations, education system, corporate governance, interfirm relations and employment relations), exhibit strong complementarity and coherence.

The salient feature of the DME variety is a strong dependence on foreign capital, while the main source of investment is foreign direct investment (FDI). Corporate governance is then dominated by the hierarchical control of transnational companies' headquarters, which becomes the central coordination mechanism in DMEs, in contrast to markets and contractual relations in LMEs or networks and associations in CMEs. According to the authors, the term "dependence" refers to the work on dependent development in South America, for example Evans (1979).

The position of employees appears to be weaker than in the coordinated market economy, because transnational corporations look for cheap but skilled labour force and may rely on the competition among post-socialist countries to attract foreign direct investments, but the labour legislation is less flexible than in the liberal market economy in order to avoid social troubles that could impede production. Therefore, a decentralized, wage bargaining organization at firm-level should become widespread in DMEs.

Tax competition and low taxation to attract FDIs result in limited government spending on education. Moreover, transnational corporations do not seem eager to invest more so as to upgrade workers' skills given the industrial specialization of the DMEs. Similarly, major investments in research and development are not necessary, while most of it is carried out within transnational companies' headquarters and then integrated into the subsidiaries production processes, innovation remaining under the control of the corporate hierarchy. The DME countries in East-Central Europe demonstrate a comparative advantage in the assembly and production of relatively complex and durable consumer goods, which are then exported. The automotive and consumer electronics sectors are particularly concerned. This comparative advantage eventually rests on the availability of a cheap but skilled labour force, technological transfers within transnational corporations and capital inflows through foreign direct investments.

Dependent market economies should not be considered as a flawed model. On the contrary, Nölke and Vliegenthart (2009, 693) believe that the post-socialist dependent capitalism in East-Central Europe is a rather "stable and fairly successful" economic model—"particularly when compared with most of the other transition countries". Institutional complementarity is the major reason explaining the coherence and stability of the model and the comparative advantage of these economies. Until the 2008 crisis (and even during the crisis), the Visegrád countries were among the best performing countries in terms of sustained economic growth and per capita GDP. The modernization of industries, technology and know-how transfer and catching-up with Western Europe can be mentioned among the positive results.

Still, the authors acknowledge the vulnerabilities and risks of this dependent type of capitalism. They underline the dependence on imported industrial goods, investment decisions of foreign-owned firms and banks, and exports to Western markets. They also point out the risk of production relocation further East by foreign investors to benefit from even cheaper labour force. They also observe the growing dualism, with rising income disparities, between workers participating in the export-oriented sectors and those who are excluded from them. Finally, they warn on the probability of Central European DMEs not being able to upgrade their economic models from their semi-peripheral position, unlike Ireland which has succeeded in catching-up with the most advanced European economies (see Figure 5.5, Chapter 5).

Nölke and Vliegenthart subscribe to a balanced vision of dependency, which does not appear to be entirely negative, since it has allowed a real modernization of industry in Central-Eastern European countries and some degree of economic catching-up. Nevertheless, they underline its shortcomings and risks, notably that of being locked into a semi-peripheral economy, dominated by foreign capital. Investment in education, research and innovation at the national level then appears as a key variable likely to help these countries to get out of this lock-in situation and to move upmarket and increase the amount of added value. This dialectical vision of dependency is reminiscent of the aforementioned "dependent development" approach by Cardoso and Faletto or Evans.

Drahokoupil & Myant (2011) also refer to a «dependent» economic model in East-Central Europe, although they prefer to qualify it as «FDI-based (second rank) market economies». Apart from the term, which they do not take up but which they do not hesitate to use anyway, they share Nölke and Vliegenthart's balanced vision of dependency. On the one hand, they acknowledge these countries' higher economic performances compared to other transition countries during the 2000s, notably due to their integration into MNCs production networks and to relatively sophisticated manufactured goods exports. Without mentioning a centre/periphery division, this integration nevertheless puts them in a second-rank position vis-à-vis Western European countries. On the other hand, they wonder whether transition economies have not missed a chance with, as a result at the end of the transition process, «a dependent status as outposts for foreign MNCs. Effectively no high-tech activities developed under domestic ownership, and MNCs brought little of their high-value activities into CEECs. The future of these economies was left uncertain, dependent on decisions made elsewhere» (Drahokoupil and Myant, 2011, 332). According to them, the missed opportunity is related to the role of the state, which should not have been reduced but on the contrary increased in education, research and infrastructure.

Unsurprisingly, the concept of dependent capitalism does not win all the votes, but the idea of dependence on FDI or foreign capital in general and a less advantageous position in international value chains are generally emphasized. This reluctance may be connected to the Marxist inspiration of dependency theories, even if, as pointed out earlier, the approach to dependent capitalism in Central and Eastern Europe has moved away from it.

Farkas (2016, 63), for example, criticizes Nölke and Vliegenthart for their essentialist view about FDI in their model of "dependent market economies": "the authors apply FDI unilaterally as a single, universal explanatory factor". However, she also acknowledges FDI's central role in the Central and Eastern European model of capitalism and in its macroeconomic dynamics during the 2000s, which led to a relative convergence with other EU countries. But this model of "modernization based on FDI" leads to a situation of "asymmetric dependence on the OMS [old member states]" (idem, 176), which is likely to persist given the institutional complementarity on which it is based, unless economic policy is oriented to develop innovation at the local level, to move up the value chain and to produce more technology-intensive goods. The early dependency theorists would probably not have disavowed this idea of "asymmetric dependency".

The Specific Context of the 2008 Crisis

If the concept of dependent capitalism is revisited in a different theoretical framework from its original one, the historical context in which it reappears, the 2008 financial crisis, is also far removed from that of Latin America in the 1960s–1970s. It participates in the renewal of the concept of dependency by revealing CEECs' vulnerabilities and asymmetrical dependency, whose outward-oriented growth models appear difficult to sustain. Its impact on these economies makes the analysis in terms of dependent capitalism even more relevant. Moreover, it highlights different forms of dependence, underlined by Drahokoupil and Myant (2011), whose combination contributes to the emergence of different national varieties of dependent capitalism and to the enlargement of the circle of East European dependent economies beyond the Visegrad Group, towards north (Baltic countries) and south (Balkans).[4]

[4] National historical trajectories from 1990 to 2020 and the different varieties of dependent capitalism will be further developed in Chapter 5.

Thus, Central-Eastern European countries represent a first type of dependent economies, at the same time strongly export- and import-oriented, and privileged host countries for foreign direct investment, as early as the 1990s. With the 2008 crisis, they had to cope with a fall in demand from Western Europe and a sharp contraction in capital inflows. The crisis effects were long-lasting and resulted notably in a slower pace of growth (Myant, 2018).

But the most affected countries by the crisis were those where financial dependency has grown strongly (Baltic countries, Southeast Europe, Hungary, Slovenia). In these countries, FDI has flowed significantly into the banking and real estate sectors, contributing to the emergence of a second type of dependent capitalism, marked by a strong financial dependence and a growth regime fuelled by plenty of credit (EBRD, 2009). Easy access to credit allowed, in particular, to support household consumption, compensating for a low level of social protection and a wage dynamics that was kept under control and below the trend in productivity gains. However, the 2008 banking crisis highlighted the dangers of this second form of dependence. The global credit crunch, followed by a capital withdrawal from Central and Eastern European countries, resulted in a liquidity crisis and a sharp depreciation of currencies under floating exchange rate regimes worsening the situation of foreign currency borrowing agents. The most exposed countries were compelled to rely on IMF and EU conditional financial assistance against austerity programs and privatization of remaining public entities. As a result, these growth models became even more dependent.

Finally, remittances can be considered to be at the root of a third type of dependency. In Europe, they mainly concern Western Balkans countries (Figure 5.4, Chapter 5). But they are also important in some new EU member states, such as Croatia, the Baltic States, Bulgaria and Romania. Remittances, mainly from Western Europe, help support domestic demand in these countries and are a source of liquidity. The 2008 crisis resulted in a decline of remittance flows from Western European countries.

Conclusion

Far from the initial formulation of dependency theories in the 1950s-1970s Latin American context, the concept of dependent capitalism reappears in the 2000s to describe the reality of post-socialist Central and Eastern European economies. It now falls within the scope of Comparative Capitalism and no longer within the legacy of Marxism and imperialism theory. Nevertheless, it shares some common elements with the original dependency approach, notably the emphasis on power struggles, coalitions and conflicts between internal and external actors from «peripheral» countries. The emergent model of capitalism in Central and Eastern Europe is characterized above all by its dependence on foreign capital, especially FDI. The model's institutional complementarity ensures a relative stability and allows some economic catching-up, but may at the same time be a source of lock-in in a semi-peripheral economic trajectory. This balanced vision is not without echoing Cardoso and Faletto's «dependent development» approach. As a new family of models, dependent capitalism can be subdivided into different national variants according to the type of capital and dependence involved (Chapter 5).

However, a number of elements, including the ambiguity between capitalism and market economy, the focus on the firm and the lack of other macroeconomic institutional forms, the emphasis on complementarity rather than institutional hierarchy, suggest that Nölke and Vligenthart's approach is constrained by the VoC analytical framework (Schedelik et al., 2021). We therefore put the emphasis on the *Régulation* theory in the present book, because as already mentioned it is a genuine theory of capitalism and its dynamics, even though the concept of dependent capitalism was initially developed in the VoC framework (Table 3.1). In particular, *Régulation* theory allows us to include other macro-institutional forms in the analysis (Delteil, 2018), starting with the monetary regime, and thereby to extend the scope of dependent capitalism to Balkan economies (Magnin & Nenovsky, 2021).

Table 3.1 Dependent market economies (DMEs) or dependent capitalism in CEECs: two analytical frameworks

VoC theoretical framework	*Dependent Market Economies (DMEs)*	*RT theoretical framework*	*Dependent Capitalism*
Coordination mechanism	Dependence on FDIs and on intrafirm hierarchies within transnational enterprises	Competition conditions	Importance of price competition, openness to foreign competition and investment, low protection against foreign firms, tax competition
Corporate governance	Control by headquarters of transnational enterprises	State	Low to moderate level of social protection, low taxation (flat tax), limited public expenditures in education, «weak states» in some countries
Industrial relations	Appeasement of skilled labour; company-level collective agreements	Monetary and financial regime	Dependent monetary regime Low sophistication of financial markets, high banking concentration, foreign ownership of banks
Education and training system	Limited expenditures for further qualification	Wage-labour nexus	Weak unionization, semi-flexible labour legislation, cheap but skilled labour force
Transfer of innovations	Intrafirm transfer within transnational enterprise	Modes of international integration	High share of exports within EU, dependence on FDI and integration into European (German) value chains, dependence on foreign financial inflows

VoC theoretical framework	*Dependent Market Economies (DMEs)*	*RT theoretical framework*	*Dependent Capitalism*
Institutional complementarity	Between activity spheres	Institutional complementarity	Between the institutional forms listed above
Institutional hierarchy	None	Institutional hierarchy	Dominance of international integration and competition, dependent monetary regime, weak state, weakened wage-labour nexus
Comparative advantages	Assembly platforms for semi-standardized industrial goods	Growth regime	Export-led growth. Financialized growth

Source Own elaboration. Nölke and Vliegenthart (2009). Varieties of capitalism (VoC). *Régulation* theory (RT)

References

Baran, P. (1957). *The political economy of growth*. Penguin Books.

Boyer, R. (1990). *The regulation school: A critical introduction*. Columbia University Press.

Bresser-Pereira, L. C. (2009). Amérique Latine: de l'interprétation nationaliste à l'interprétation par la dépendance. *Revue Tiers Monde, 199*(July–September), 533–546.

Cardoso, F. H. (1977). The consumption of dependency theory in the United States. *Latin American Research Review, 12*(3), 7–24.

Cardoso, F. H., & Faletto, E. (1979). *Dependency and development in Latin America*. University of California Press.

Delteil, V. (2018). Capitalismes dépendants d'Europe centrale et orientale: pièges de la dépendance externe et instrumentations domestiques. *Revue de la régulation* [On Line], 24 | 2nd semester/Autumn.

Dos Santos, T. (1970). The structure of dependence. *American Economic Review, 60*(2), 231–236.

Drahokoupil, J., & Myant, M. (2011). *Transition economies: Political economy in Russia, Eastern Europe, and Central Asia*. Wiley.

Ebenau, M., Bruff, I., & May, C. (2015). *New directions in comparative capitalisms research. Critical and global perspectives*. Palgrave Macmillan.

EBRD. (2009). *Transition report: Transition in crisis?* European Bank for Reconstruction and Development.

Evans, P. (1979). *Dependent development: The alliance of multinational, state, and local capital in Brazil*. Princeton University Press.

Farkas, B. (2016). *Models of capitalism in the European Union*. Palgrave Macmillan.

Frank, A. G. (1967). *Capitalism and underdevelopment in Latin America*. Monthly Review Press.

Furtado, C. (1965). Development and stagnation in Latin America: A structuralist approach. *Studies in Comparative International Development, 1*(11), 159–175.

Girvan, N. (1973). The development of dependency economics in the Caribbean and Latin America: Review and comparison. *Social and Economic Studies, 22*(1), 1–33.

Hall, P., & Soskice, D. (Eds.). (2001). *Varieties of capitalism: The institutional foundations of comparative advantage*. Oxford University Press.

Hilferding, R. (1910 [1981]). *Finance capital. A study of the latest phase of capitalist development*. Routledge and Kegan Paul.

Hobson, J. (1902). *Imperialism. A study*. James Pott & Company.

King, L. (2002). Postcommunist divergence: A comparative analysis of the transition to capitalism in Poland and Russia. *Studies in Comparative International Development, 37*(3), 3–34.

Lenin, V. I. (1917 [1999]). *Imperialism: The highest stage of capitalism.* Resistance books.
Luxemburg, R. (1913 [2003]). *The accumulation of capital.* Routledge.
Magnin, E., Delteil, V., & Vercueil, J. (2018). La dépendance dans les relations entre capitalismes nationaux: quelle portée analytique? *Revue de la Régulation* [on line], 24, 2nd semester/Autumn.
Magnin, E., & Nenovsky, N. (2021). Dependent monetary regimes in the Balkans: Enlarging the "variety of capitalism" hypothesis. *International Journal of Public Administration, 44*(14), 1216–1230.
May, C., & Nölke, A. (2018). Dangers of residual dependency in state-permeated capitalism: The case of Brazil during labor party rule. *Revue de la Régulation* [on line], 24, 2nd semester/Autumn.
Myant, M. (2018). The limits to dependent growth in East-Central Europe. *Revue de la Régulation* [on line], 24, 2nd semester/Autumn.
Nölke, A., & Vliegenthart, A. (2009). Enlarging the variety of capitalism: The emergence of dependent market economies in East Central Europe. *World Politics, 61*(4), 670–702.
Schedelik, M., Nölke, A., Mertens, D., & May, C. (2021). Comparative capitalism, growth models and emerging markets: The development of the field. *New Political Economy, 26*(4), 514–526.
Stark, D. (1992). Path dependence and privatization strategies in East Central Europe. *East European Politics and Societies, 6*(1), 17–54.
Sunkel, O. (1969). National development policy and external dependence in Latin America. *The Journal of Development Studies, 6*(1), 23–48.
Sunkel, O. (1973). Transnational capitalism and national disintegration in Latin America. *Social and Economic Studies, 22*(1), 132–176.
Wallerstein, I. (1974). *The modern world-system I: Capitalist agriculture and the origins of the European world-economy in the sixteenth century.* Academic Press.

CHAPTER 4

Dependent Monetary Regime

Abstract This chapter presents the theory of DMR and its place in the institutional configuration of dependent capitalism. The monetary regime is defined as "a set of formal rules of monetary behaviour, as well as mechanisms of their enforcement', consisting of two main components—internal (monetary policy regime) and external (exchange rate regime). The main characteristics of DMR are presented, namely passive and liberal exchange rate regime and monetary policy, limited LOLR, low levels of seigniorage, etc. The basic DMR institutional forms and their sustainability are also discussed. Special attention is paid to the Currency board (limited or complete lack of monetary discretion) and euroization (absence of national currency). These two DMRs are compared with the pegged and adjustable exchange rate regimes of a Central Bank pursuing a discretionary monetary policy.

Keywords Exchange rates regime · Monetary policy regime · Dependent monetary regime · Currency substitution · Currency board · Monetary union · Euroization

E. Magnin and N. Nenovsky, *Diversity of Capitalism in Central and Eastern Europe*, https://doi.org/10.1007/978-3-031-04950-7_4

Monetary Dependence: General Perspective

For the purpose of reflecting on the subject, we will define monetary regime as a "set of formal rules of monetary behaviour, as well as mechanisms of their enforcement" (Magnin & Nenovsky, 2021).[1] Within the monetary regime, two components (sub-regimes) can be distinguished—internal and external—which often conflict with each other.

The first, external component (external rules) we can call "exchange rate regime" (ERR). It covers the legal rules of exchange rate formation (through the market or through monetary authorities' interventions), as well as the mechanisms of convertibility of national currency into foreign currency (from full convertibility to full control). Albeit often overlooked in the analysis of the exchange rate mechanism, convertibility is an essential component of it (Guillaumont-Jeanneney, 2015). The degree of convertibility can be linked to the "quality" of national currency. Higher convertibility means higher currency "quality" (Schuler, 1999).[2]

The second, internal component of the monetary regime (internal monetary rules), can be referred to as "monetary policy regime" (MPR). Monetary policy is related to the influence on the monetary base, on money supply in general (this includes domestic credit), on liquidity and generally on GDP domestic components. Monetary policy is associated with the interest rate policy (i.e. with the different channels of transmission mechanisms), and nowadays with quantitative and qualitative easing and the active management of the yield curve. Monetary policy can be discretional or conducted according to pre-set rules (rule of full coverage of the monetary base with foreign exchange assets, rule of monetary aggregate growth, Taylor's rule, "Central Bank (CB) loss function" and CB response function', and so on, and so forth). Some configurations incorporate rules whereby the internal component of the monetary

[1] We follow the familiar definition of institution made by D. North (1990a; b), for details see Desquilbet and Nenovsky (2004), Nenovsky and Rizopoulos (2003).

[2] Schuler defines "type of exchange rate" and "type of monetary authority". With regard to the type of exchange rate, a distinction is made between: fixed, controlled and floating, and with the type of monetary authority: discretionary authority and rule-bound authority. The rule-bound authority in turn falls into: Currency boards, quasi-currency boards, private Central Banks, absence of national monetary authority, temporary monetary authority, etc. (Schuler, 1999). Convertibility is often cited as a major advantage of Currency boards (Coats, 2007).

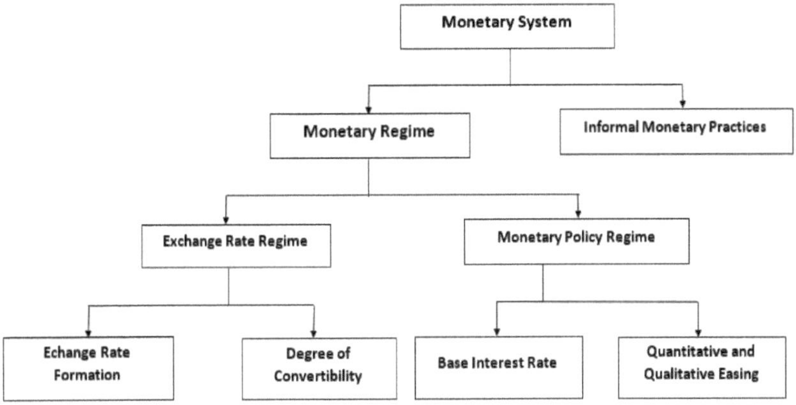

Fig. 4.1 Structure of the monetary system (*Source* the authors)

regime—monetary policy—is completely eliminated, such as the Currency board and dollarization.

If we add to the monetary regime (consisting of these two components) the informal rules of monetary behaviour (those arising from the traditions and monetary practices of the population and economic agents), we come to the definition of the "monetary system" of a given country (Fig. 4.1).

We will clarify that monetary behaviour encompasses the economic agents participating in a given monetary payment community (in this case the nation state) and is linked to the processes of measurement, calculation, accounting, payment and saving (the enumeration follows the familiar functions of money).

Monetary regime, i.e. the formal, codified monetary relations reflect the power relationships, economic interests and strategies of the key political and economic actors or groups of actors.[3] Power relationships are manifested both within monetary communities and among monetary communities. Actors can be grouped in different ways subject to the needs of the analysis and the research context (external/internal, debtors/creditors, by sector, etc.). History has shown it many times: the

[3] Informal monetary institutions also represent conflicts of interest and power asymmetries. The specifics of the manifestation of power and economic conflicts in formal and informal monetary rules are not the subject of analysis in this study.

change of the monetary regime goes hand in hand with the change of the political regime, the monetary crisis is also a political crisis.[4] Deep, systemic political changes are accompanied by radical, systemic monetary changes. Such was, for example, the transition from a communist planning system to a market capitalist one in the former Eastern European countries, including the Balkans.

From the standpoint of the study, i.e. of the "dependent monetary regime (DMR)", it is particularly important to distinguish between national and foreign actors, including national and foreign monetary authorities (Central Banks). This analytical differentiation is important because, most generally, a country's monetary regime is an extension of its geopolitical and geoeconomic place in the international system. Structurally, the political, military and economic power hierarchy, the relationship of dominance among individual nation-states within the world economy (cf Chapter 3), determine and actively interact with the hierarchy of national money. Political and economic sovereignty go hand in hand with monetary sovereignty.[5] The literature and the press often feature the existence of a "monetary pyramid" and a "hierarchical and de-territorial monetary geography" (B. Cohen's research, 1998, 2015[6], is especially important in this regard). The monetary pyramid actually reflects the hierarchy, the relations of dominance in the pyramid of economic power of individual countries. In a similar vein, de Bernis writes:

> "The money of the dominant production system is not only dominant money, it is presented as 'world money'. [...] There is dominant money, that of the dominant production system in a world of heterogeneous money". (de Bernis, 1987, 925, 934)

Furthermore, ever since its birth the world capitalist economy has developed as a dynamic, i.e. changing, hierarchical system, displaying cyclical phases of different periodicity and character. The pyramid changes its structure, especially at its top layers—those of the leading currencies.

[4] See, for example, Aglietta and Orléan (1982).

[5] Helleiner (2003), Lo Vuolo and Pereira (2018).

[6] "Monetary space" and the concepts of "dominance", "monetary dominance" including, are concepts introduced by François Perroux and D. de Bernis (B. Cohen notes the pioneering role of Perroux).

The monetary system and monetary regime of smaller countries follow these cyclical patterns. Of particular importance, are the alternating phases of globalization and de-globalization (national or regional), which are accompanied by the alteration of international monetary regimes with national (regional) ones (more specifically 'monetary nationalism'). In the modern monetary world, the place of national money in the hierarchy of money and credit is manifested also through their suitability to be used in different swaps lines (exchange of national currency) between national CBs (Mehrling, 2015). After the dollar, the swaps lines among the six biggest Central Banks are the second most important liquidity instrument today. After then came the bilateral swaps with other "less important" CBs. The Chinese CB is particularly active in this field signing multiple swaps lines with many CBs.

It follows from the foregoing that the dynamic monetary dependence/independence of a particular country is a direct continuation of, as well as "serving", the (geo)political and economic dependence/independence of that country.[7] We will see further these relations manifesting in the modern monetary systems of the Balkan countries, i.e. in the post-communist period, after 1990 (Chapters 6 and 7). Still, they are rooted in a long-term historical perspective, dating back to the end of the nineteenth century (Magnin & Nenovsky, 2022). The historical perspective is particularly interesting. It shows how the alteration of the leading centres of attraction (geopolitical and economic) also determines the nature of the Balkan monetary regimes.

How is the subordination, the dependence of the monetary regime explained on a more specific level? From the onset we should emphasize that a dependent monetary regime, as in dependent capitalism in general, can be successful systems (under certain conditions), and overall the practice shows that they are such because they take into account the structural realities of the international order. In this sense, our analysis is not normative in nature and "dependence" does not carry a negative connotation to us. It is an analytical concept.[8]

[7] The Digital Dollar Project writes: "If payment systems could bypass Western banks heavily linked economically and geopolitically to US dollar reserves, the effectiveness of economic sanctions as a central and unifying tool of our foreign policy would be at serious risk" (White, 2020).

[8] Monetary dependence has been interpreted and can be interpreted within the framework of various theoretical approaches to economic development (see for Africa,

Small and peripheral countries are catching-up in their economic development (by different quantitative and qualitative criteria). As a rule, they are geopolitically dependent of low economic and military "weight"; their elites are unable to unite around a common goal, and they have no effective internal governance mechanisms in place (Cohen, 2015). Their general domestic institutional and political instability are crucial, and it makes the monetary regime highly vulnerable to fluctuations in the political cycle and conflicts of interest, power struggles, corruption, etc. The monetary regime is dominated by fiscal policy. Often DMRs are born after military conflicts, or after financial and monetary crises, after a severe crisis of statehood. The political instability is even more pronounced in systemic changes (such as those experienced by former communist countries).[9]

To overcome falling behind economically, these countries need specific institutions and mechanisms.[10] These institutions and factors are not many. Apart from the central role of the state, the "role of external capital" is also present, be it in direct investments or in the form of debt. The need for external capital is dictated by insufficient domestic savings, and the generally low technological level and limited competitive export opportunities. Peripheral and dependent countries cannot borrow on international markets debt denominated in their own national currencies ("original sin hypothesis"). They borrow in major world currencies and become vulnerable to currency (exchange rate) risk. The inflow of external capital, in turn, requires a corresponding stable institutional and political environment. A leading condition for foreign capital, as well as for the involvement of foreign financial institutions, in addition to

Dixon-Fyle, 1978), some of which have been presented in Chapter 3. Without providing an overview, we will note the different contemporary approaches of Marxism (A. Emmanuel, S. Amin, G. Arrighi), of the "world-economy" (O. Cox, E. Wallerstein), of the Latin American structuralists (R. Prebisch, C. Furtado, D. Prates, R. Lo Vuolo, JM. Pereira), of F. Perroux and the Grenoble school (G. de Bernis), of modern international political economy, etc. Most approaches "condemn" this dependency, but it can be viewed in a purely positive light, for example, by supporters of "realism" in international political economy, monetarists (M. Friedman, R. Mandel, H. Johnson, S. Hanke, among others), etc. In our text we have followed our own generalizations, in particular observations of real monetary processes.

[9] See overview of the theoretical approaches to monetary regimes in "economies in transition" (Grittersová, 2014).

[10] Interesting in this respect are, for instance, the contributions of A. Gerschenkron (1962) on the role of catching-up institutions and the "theory of import institutions", to name a few.

favourable tax conditions, is the introduction of a monetary regime that could ensure the return on this capital and its predictability. This implies a low level of risk (currency and political). It follows that the monetary regimes of the peripheral and catching-up countries are built in a way that suits the political and geopolitical interests of the leading capital centres. The political regimes in the dependent countries can be viewed in a way similar to that of the monetary regime (they must be stable and loyal to the geopolitical centre and their financial institutions).

We should note once again that dependence does not mean that small countries do not benefit from this type of monetary and political regimes; on the contrary—in most cases it is the most appropriate, so to speak, "optimal" form which, if skilfully managed, minimizes losses under a given external structural constraint. Whenever attempts were made to introduce a stand-alone independent monetary regime (floating or pegged), in the presence of geopolitical dependence, they were unsuccessful and generally ended in a financial and political crisis.

Therefore, the external equilibrium (external stability), i.e. the state of the balance of payments and especially its financial (capital) account, as well as the dynamics of the exchange rate, become central parameters for the development of the peripheral countries. Also, we know from national accounting that the balance of payments is linked to the monetary sector and is a source of money supply. As a rule, in dependent countries, external sources of money supply dominate domestic sources (domestic credit, for example). The monetary regime of the small, peripheral and catching-up economies is directed outwards. It is international in nature and in most cases its definition and management are delegated to the leading centre. The dependent monetary regime includes a strict (rigorous) monetary policy (rule-bound), which follows that of the centre, as well as the pegging of the national currency to that of the leading centre (or the complete abandonment of the national currency[11]). Milton Friedman calls them "unified currency" regimes (Friedman, 1973).

[11] Fixed exchange rates, free convertibility and the observance of externally set rules are considered manifestation of "monetary internationalism", while floating and controlled exchange rates and discretionary policy, pursuing domestic economic targets are considered "monetary nationalism". This principled distinction is presented in the pioneering book of M. Heilperin (Heilperin, 1939). Similar ideas were developed in Schuler (1999).

Here, it is appropriate to add that when considering the diversity of capitalism, Drahokoupil and Myant (2011) define the ways of financing the current account of the countries from Eastern Europe, i.e. their integration into the world economy as a key criterion for determining the differences in the trajectories of post-communist capitalisms (the authors define a total of six such trajectories).[12] However, the authors do not elaborate the topic of the monetary regime, which, in our opinion, is closely linked to the international integration of these countries (see Chapter 2).

Furthermore, the restrictive monetary regime can exist in a comprehensive institutional matrix, encompassing rules on public finances (fiscal conservatism and low disproportionate taxes), on the labour market (its flexibility, weak unions, etc.), on the industrial structure (dependence on transnational corporation located in Western countries), on the financial system (the presence of branches of foreign banks, dependent on their Western parent banks), etc. (see Magnin, 2020; Magnin & Nenovsky, 2021; also Table 2, Chapter 3). The concept of institutional complementarity presented in Chapter 2 is most relevant here. A simplified graphic representation of the institutional matrix, i.e. institutional complementarity, is given in Fig. 4.2.

Finally, it is interesting to add that the imposition of a dependent regime in small and peripheral countries is accompanied by the imposition and dissemination of economic views, theories and ideas ("economic narrative"), which legitimize this new monetary regime and prepare the imposition of a certain economic development model. Moreover, as a rule, the development of economic thought in dependent countries follows that of the centre around which the country gravitates (Marinova & Nenovsky, 2019).[13] In this sense, one can speak of the existence of a certain "intellectual dependence" (a kind of "soft power"). For example, in the 1930s, "corporatist ideas" and "clearing payment theories" were popular among Bulgarians due to German and Italian influence. After World War II, these were the socialist ideas and Soviet "anti-monetary theories" because of USSR influence. The following

[12] It is worth noting that as early as 1979, A. Thirnwall linked the specifics of the monetary regime with the nature of the current account.

[13] See also Nenovsky and Penchev (2015), and Nenovsky and Mihaylova-Borisova (2015).

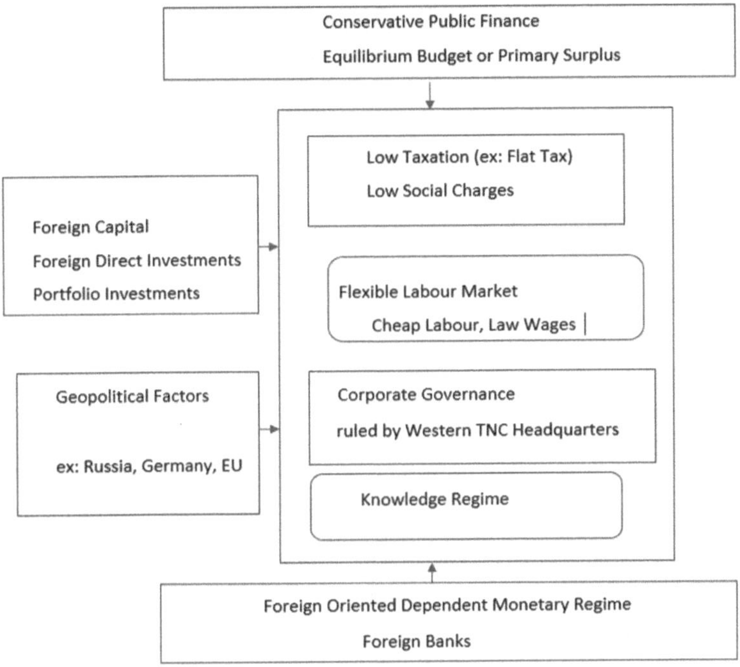

Fig. 4.2 Dependent capitalism: institutional matrix and interconnections (*Source* the authors)

Chapters 6 and 7 present a number of examples from Balkan countries' post-socialist monetary history.[14]

Elements of Dependent Monetary Regimes

If we limit ourselves to purely economic dimensions (as far as they can be separated from the (geo)political ones), dependent monetary regime is characterized by the following main characteristics.

First, *with regard to the exchange rate regime (ERR),* a passive and liberal exchange rate policy is followed. By their nature, these regimes are

[14] On the cycles of monetary dependence in the Balkans, since the nineteenth century going hand in hand with the dominance of certain economic and monetary ideas, one may refer to Magnin and Nenovsky (2022).

international. Most often, a fixed exchange rate is resorted to, or pegged to a foreign anchor currency (the currency of a leading country, primarily the dollar, or a basket of leading currencies). This is accompanied by free convertibility. This choice is accompanied by the accumulation of significant foreign reserves, which guarantee the chosen level of the exchange rate. Foreign exchange reserves are invested in highly liquid assets, gold and most often debt securities of the country whose currency is chosen as an anchor. The aim is to ensure the convertibility of the national currency, as well as to reduce currency risk.[15] Within passive exchange rate regimes (as we will see below), a legally fixed coverage of the monetary base with highly liquid foreign assets (Currency board regime)[16] is often added.

In another configuration, the national currency is completely abandoned as legal tender, i.e. a foreign currency is accepted as such (Schobert, 2003). In this case, we are talking about unilateral dollarization or euroization. In this configuration, foreign exchange reserves are significantly lower (they only serve to pay off debt and finance imports), but are initially spent on the purchase of dollar (or euro) banknotes. Participation in a common monetary union can also be seen as a passive and dependent regime, in so far as a small country does not have a serious influence on the common monetary policy.

In any case, although to a different degree, the monetary sovereignty of the dependent country is limited or completely abolished: it is delegated to foreign monetary authorities. This abandonment of monetary sovereignty is manifested in the basic functions of money, first abandoning the national means of saving, then the function of payment and finally the unit of measurement.

Secondly, in the above connection, we can also note the consequences of the dependent regime in terms of *competitiveness*, often identified with the dynamics of the real exchange rate. It is true that the tendency is for the national currency to appreciate, which, when productivity increases insufficiently, leads to a reduced competitiveness of exports, to an increase in imports, and as a result to deterioration of the current account. The appreciation of national money comes along different lines, but mostly due to higher growth rates of national prices and wages compared

[15] This way, a specific mechanism is reached, whereby national resources are transferred to the centre, as the resources that could be used in a national economy are invested in foreign financial assets (Schwartz, 1993, 170).

[16] Or quasi-currency board, depending on the percentage of coverage and the percentage of domestic assets on the balance sheet.

to those in the anchor country (catching-up effect known as Balassa-Samuelson). The appreciation of the exchange rate causes an inflow of capital, which generally compensates for the current account deficit. However, they make the system unsustainable, which in turn requires conservative public finances (balanced budget and low domestic debt), as well as a restriction on domestic credit. Of course, this appreciation of the national currency depends on the geographical structure of exports, and there are mechanisms that work in the opposite direction, deterring the appreciation. Among them, for example, is the "discipline effect", which, in the absence of devaluation, forces economic agents to become more productive (Nenovsky et al., 2001).

Third, where it exists, the internal component of the monetary regime, that of *monetary policy (MPR)* (mostly interest rate policy), is also forced to passively follow the monetary policy movement of the anchor CB. The monetary base and the money supply in general are determined endogenously by the demand for money, and the money supply passively adapts to demand. Thus, the monetary authorities of the small country find it difficult to also control the domestic sources of money supply. This passivity is expressed not only by the automatic following of the anchor-CB interest rate, but also by the fact that foreign banks dominate the banking system, i.e. they determine the dynamics and conditions of the money and credit market (and its possible vulnerability due to the movement of speculative capital within these banking groups, between headquarters and branches of these banks, credit bubbles, etc., Nenovsky & Villieu, 2011). The interbank market and liquidity in dependent countries also reflect the dynamics of international markets. This is a further constraint on national sovereignty, because systemic banks have foreign capital and can be a tool for promoting foreign strategic interests. The payment system is also closely linked to the leading economies (in some cases it is outside the country, such as at the beginning in Estonia).[17]

Fourth, from what has been said, it follows that *the financial stability framework* has obvious limitations. The LOLR (lender of last resort) function is either minimized (Currency board) or completely eliminated

[17] The payment system is particularly important in dependent regimes, the example of the crisis in dollarized Panama is illustrative. Some countries in the former Yugoslavia (Bosnia and Herzegovina, for example), whose payment systems were in Belgrade, had similar problems.

(dollarization). Of course, it can be assumed that, under certain conditions, in a liquidity crisis, foreign banks will be refinanced from outside, through their "parent banks" (and respectively from the foreign CB). Practice shows that most often this does not happen. A system of deposit insurance and banking supervision remains in the hands of national monetary authorities (often banking regulations can be used as a monetary policy instrument).[18] It is important to add here that various mechanisms can possibly fulfil the role of LOLR, such as the Banking Department in Bulgaria, protection swaps, formal or informal arrangements with anchor CBs, agreement with the IMF, as well as ad hoc mechanisms such as the Vienna Initiatives of 2009 and 2012 (where 15 Western banks, with the participation of a number of monetary financial institutions (MFIs), pledged support to their subsidiaries in Emerging Europe)[19], etc.

Fifth, as a general result of the above characteristics, a country with a dependent monetary regime partially or completely loses control over its *internal adjustments* (at the expense of *external adjustments* and stability), it can neither "postpone them" nor "pass them onto other countries" and actors. It can "postpone" them at the expense of the IMF, but against certain reforms. And to "postpone and pass on adjustments" according to Cohen (2015) are the main manifestations of "monetary power". The opposite takes place: foreign disequilibria are transferred to dependent countries, and these countries are forced to react with internal and national mechanisms (for example, austerity policy). As already mentioned, within banking groups, resources can be transferred from dependent countries toward banking centres. Furthermore, it can be assumed that when the response in a peripheral country is by way of restrictiveness, an authoritarian and generally forceful, political regime becomes most effective.

Generally speaking, the monetary power of small countries is extremely limited: they have neither power resources (political, military, financial, etc.), nor can they influence the behaviour or shape the preferences of other countries ("monetary power as a relation") (Nenovsky, 2007). The asymmetry in the international power space of money, in fact, is not

[18] However, under certain conditions, they may also be limited. For example, from October 1, 2020, Bulgaria and Croatia join the EU Banking Union without being part of the euro area. Thus, the national Central Banks of both countries lose control over the leading and systemic banks.

[19] http://vienna-initiative.com/.

new—it has been a characteristic feature since the time of the international gold mine; it existed in the late nineteenth century until World War I, where creditor countries dominated (Simmons, 1996).

Sixth, we can add that under the dependent monetary regime, the sources of monetary income (seigniorage) shrink because a large part of the money supply is in foreign currency.[20] We will recall that the seigniorage can be divided into two components: (i) monetary seigniorage (income of the Central Bank received from the issue of banknotes and coins) and (ii) bank seigniorage (income of the Central Bank received from the transformation of maturities). With banking seigniorage, the Central Bank performs the functions of a normal financial intermediary (it profits from a positive difference between the return on financial assets and its non-monetary liabilities). Under dependent monetary regimes, bank seigniorage is practically very limited or zero, and may even be negative (in an attempt to pursue an active monetary policy).[21]

Finally, in a regime of dollarization and euroization, when the dollar and the euro circulate as official currency, we can also speak of leaving the *"symbolic" sovereignty*. Money is part of the symbols of any sovereign national government (Heilleiner, 2003). As we have known since the time of the "father" of the sovereignty theory, Jean Bodin, the right to mint coins and receive income from it is an inalienable part of the rights of every sovereign, be it a monarch in the past or the people (nation today) (in the face of the state and CB).[22] However, we must make the proviso that the classical monetary sovereignty is becoming increasingly difficult to implement in today's global and interdependent world. It becomes necessary for the monetary sovereignty to become cooperative and shared. The subsidiarity principle is even more frequently applied in the monetary sphere (Zimmermann, 2013). According to some authors, the monetary sovereignty however can be regarded also as a continuously developing

[20] For discussion see Fischer (1982), Schobert (2003), and a number of articles of the latter.

[21] The case of Lebanon is similar, as are the losses of the Central Bank in the financial crisis of 2019 (see Nenovsky and Chobanov, 2020). Under the dependent regime, the inflation tax is also eliminated (Hanke, 2002a, b, Hanke speaks of an inflationary component of seigniorage).

[22] See Helleiner (2003). The issue of monetary sovereignty and seigniorage is disputed during the choice between a Currency board or euroization in Kosovo and Bosnia and Herzegovina (Coats, 2007).

system of values as regards money and the monetary system, marked by the historical context and national specificities.[23]

Institutional Formsof the Dependent Monetary Regime

We have already mentioned that monetary dependence is manifested primarily in relation to the monetary regime (although it also has a place in informal monetary practices, the familiar process of "monetary, currency substitution"). In an order of increasing dependence, we can distinguish the following forms of monetary regimes.

(i) *Fixed (pegged) exchange rate* regime (various configurations are possible here).[24] Convertibility can vary in degree, but in general dependent regimes have wide convertibility. The elements of monetary policy (especially sterilization) are minimized, and if there is such, it closely follows the course of the monetary policy of the leading country. Monetary policy has a pre-set framework due to the relationship between the balance of payments and the monetary sector. In this configuration there is, albeit limited, a space for LOLR. What remains is deposit insurance and a scope for banking supervision. Any active monetary policy in a fixed exchange rate regime, regardless of the degree of convertibility, sooner or later leads to imbalances (disequilibria), and this results in crises and devaluations or control and a parallel foreign exchange market. There is a contradiction between the two components of the monetary regime—internal (MPR) and external (ERR), see Fig. 4.1. According to Kurt Schuler and Steve Hanke:

> Discretionary monetary authorities such as central banks have generally been unsuccessful at maintaining rigid exchange rates because they have done so in an inconsistent way. An analysis of the supply and demand for money shows the contradiction in using sterilised intervention to simultaneously target the exchange rate

[23] Also, Zimmermann (2013).

[24] According to the IMF, pegged rates are: conventional peg, stabilized arrangements, crawling peg, crawl-like arrangements and pegged with horizontal bands (IMF, 2020).

> and the nominal supply of money, as almost all central banks do sometimes and many do most of the time. (Schuler, 1999, 85)

> Pegged rates invariably result in conflicts between exchange rate policies and monetary polies. [...] Balance-of-payments crises erupt as a monetary authority increasingly offsets the reduction in the foreign component of the monetary base with domestically created base money. (Hanke, 2002a, 91)

(ii) *Currency board*, which is a comprehensive system of rules both in terms of exchange rate (ERR) and in terms of domestic money supply (MPR). In addition to legally fixing the exchange rate to a stable major currency, there is also a legal 100% (or less) coverage of the monetary base and of the main liabilities of the Central Bank, with highly liquid foreign exchange assets. Convertibility is complete.[25] In this case, the balance sheet of the Central Bank, as a rule, eliminates domestic sources of monetary base, and completely abandons the active monetary policy. The monetary base is determined endogenously by the demand for money[26] (Hanke, 2002a). In this configuration, the CB cannot influence the liquidity in the system, just as it cannot perform open market operations (OMO) or act as a LOLR (i.e. moral hazard and "principal-agent" problem are limited), etc. The balance sheet of the Central Bank or of the Currency board (Issue Department within the Central Bank) is published weekly or monthly. In each particular national case, residual liquidity impact options may be found, but these are rather exceptions. The Currency board is considered sustainable (viable) due to the strong "credibility/trust effect" (carried by the anchor currency) and as a consequence of the "discipline effect" and the systemic nature of tight budgetary constraints (see for details Desquilbet & Nenovsky, 2004). Theoretically, unlike controlled exchange rates, there is no contradiction between the

[25] According to Guillaumont-Jeanneney (2015, 34–36), the Currency board is an administratively set exchange rate, unlike other fixed exchange rate regimes, where the Central Bank intervenes. The Currency board is generally well received by the IMF because it helps implement its stabilization programs. It is often run by a foreigner (e.g. Bosnia and Herzegovina).

[26] The demand for quasi-money, in principle, i.e. not only under a Currency board, is endogenous.

two components of the monetary regime in the Currency board (Schuler, 1999). It is interesting to note that M. Friedman, who is often considered as the guru of floating exchange rates, actually preferred Currency boards (or as he calls them "unified currency") for small and peripheral economies.[27]

> "[A] unified currency assures a maximum degree of integration of the country in question with the greater world. [...] So I believe there is no conflict between wholehearted advocacy of floating rates for major countries and the existence of currency blocs of smaller countries attached to the major countries." (Edwards, 2020, pp. 14–15)

According to an in-depth study by S. Edwards, Friedman was the progenitor of the bipolar model of monetary regimes, which was later adopted by the IMF (Fischer, 2001).

> Friedman's had two preferred monetary and exchange rate arrangements for the poorer countries: flexible exchange rates, where market forces determined the value of the currency at every moment in time, and a unified currency regime, where the exchange rate is irrevocably fixed and the central bank is abolished. (Edwards, 2020, 18)

In practice, there are various institutional departures from the classical principles of a Currency board (mostly 100% coverage of the monetary base, etc.) (Camillieri Gilson, 2002; Nenovsky et al., 2001). These departures from the principles, and especially attempts to lead to a financial crisis[28] (Hanke, 2002a). However, it should be noted that unlike the colonial versions of Currency boards (often called first generation), today the movement of capital is leading and creates some instability, both in the direction of speculative credit growth and rapid withdrawal in a crisis (see Box 1) This also applies to the next form—dollarization. This instability can occur both through the banking system (Gedeon,

[27] Friedman also proposed this model during his visit to socialist Yugoslavia in March 1973 (see Chapter 6).

[28] The case of Argentina.

2013) and through other types of external capital inflows, such as EU funds (Nenovsky & Villieu, 2011; Nenovsky et al., 2013).

(iii) *Dollarization, euroization*, i.e. systems where a foreign currency is officially adopted as legal tender, and the national currency is completely abolished (with certain exceptions where small-value national coins circulate) (Schobert, 2003). In this extremely dependent monetary form, monetary authorities do exist, however they can only provisionally be called Central Bank (e.g. the Central Bank of Montenegro, Fabris et al., 2004). Convertibility is complete. There is no monetary policy. It is necessary to put foreign currency banknotes into circulation, which is done by a one-time conversion of foreign reserves into banknotes or their purchase. This regime completely links the dynamics of monetary processes with those of the leading centres and is extremely disciplining for public finances. Most often, this regime is imposed from outside, by external economic and political forces.

Box 1: Price level determination under the Gold Standard (GS) and Modern Currency board (CB)

If we extend Kydland and Wynne (2002) presentation of the GS, we could present the GS and CB price level determination as follow. First assume that the supply of money M^S is given by: $M^S = \frac{1}{\lambda} eF$, where $0 < \lambda \leq 1$ is the degree of coverage of the inside money by outside money, e is the nominal price at which the monetary authority stands willing to buy and sell the outside money, F is the stock of outside money which evolves according to the difference between exportations X and importations IMP: $\Delta F = X - IMP$. The demand for money is given by: $M^D = f(\pi^e, z)\ Py$, where π^e is expected inflation, z is a vector of other variables determined demand for money, P is general price level and y is real income.

If we suppose money market equilibrium ($M^D = M^S$) we can obtain the price level under GS as:

$$P = \frac{eF}{\lambda f(\pi^e, z)y} = \frac{e\sum(X - IMP)}{\lambda f(\pi^e, z)y} \tag{4.1}$$

Under the CB (especially second generation) there are some important structural changes: (i) the coverage exist only for the base money, not the all monetary stock (ii) with the development of the bank money, nowadays the monetary stock is far bigger that the money in circulation (this stresses the role of the banking system and the role of money multiplayer) and (iii) nowadays the capital account presents a key part of the balance of payments, while in the previous time the balance of payment was closer to the trade account. Let $M^S = \mu H$, where H is the monetary base, and μ is the money multiplayer, assume that only H is covered by F. Taking into account the role of capital flows in the determination of the stock of outside money, let $\Delta F = X - IMP + \Delta K$, where ΔK represents net capital flows. In turn $\Delta K = \Delta K_{FDI} + \Delta K_{FDIS} + \Delta K_{DEBT}$,where ΔK_{FDI} is a sustainable FDI, ΔK_{FDIS} is FDI in speculative sectors and ΔK_{DEBT} *is* debt capital.

We obtain the price level under CB:

$$P = \frac{\mu e \sum(X - IMP + \Delta KFDI + \Delta KFDIS + \Delta KDEBT)}{\lambda f(\pi^e, z)y} \tag{4.2}$$

Comparing (1) and (2) it is obvious that the price level determination is much more instable under CB because of the two behavioural variables such as money multiplayer μ and net capital flows ΔK, especially ΔK_{FDIS} and ΔK_{DEBT}.

Source: Desquilbet and Nenovsky (2004, 22) and update

(iv) Finally, ***membership in a Monetary Union.*** At first glance, this monetary form differs from those already enumerated in that it allows national "participation" in a common active monetary policy. There is a talk of "shared monetary sovereignty", where the small country is involved in monetary policy decisions. Formally, the small country owns the LOLR and receives part of the monetary income, seigniorage. It must be said that these advantages are illusory. An important condition for successful participation in a common area is the synchronous movement of the cycle of the dependent country with the cycle of the anchor country, which is rarely achieved, as well as symmetry of shocks. The common monetary policy is pursued in the interests of the leading countries, which dominate politically and economically that union. It follows the objectives and interests of the major countries in the monetary

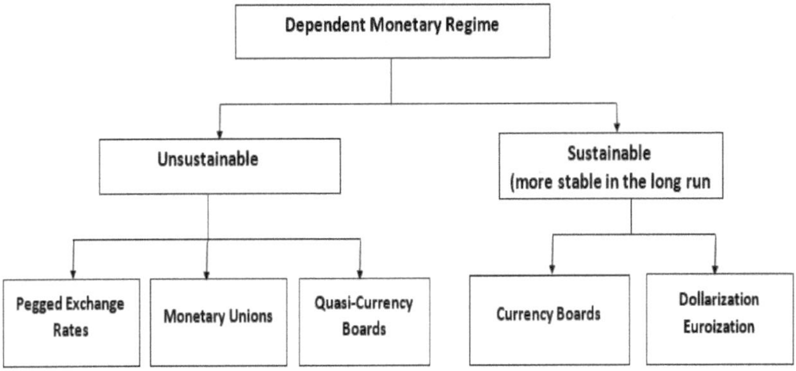

Fig. 4.3 Dependent monetary regimes (*Source* the authors)

> union or of the group interests associated with those countries. The experience of the few monetary unions of the past, as well as of those existing today, demonstrates this. An important feature, often left out of the field of analysis, is the choice of ERR for the whole area. For example, the euro area chooses a floating exchange rate, the CFA zone a fixed one, and the Caribbean Monetary Union operates as a Currency board.

With all conditionalities, within the summary of dependent configurations (Fig. 4.3), we can outline two groups: depending on whether there is a contradiction between the two components of monetary policy or if they are in sync, the former being highly volatile whereas the latter are relatively more sustainable and longer lasting. The former include various types of pegged arrangements, the latter—Currency boards and dollarization. The monetary union is somewhere midway.

This list of institutional configurations is most often viewed from the standpoint of conventional monetary "theory of optimal monetary zones" and "the choice of optimal exchange rate regime" (for arbitrage "costs/benefits", "credibility/flexibility", etc.).[29] Without denying their benefits, the above approaches cannot explain the emergence of dependent monetary regimes. Political and geopolitical factors are leading and

[29] Mongelli (2002).

this has been shown many times. For example, the choice of Currency board regimes in the Baltic countries in the early 1990s, and later the German mark as official legal tender in Montenegro, was a visible manifestation of the desire of the national elites, as well as the external centres[30], to replace the geopolitical anchor: in the first case to replace Russia with Germany and the EU, and in the second—Yugoslavia (Serbia) with Germany.[31] International political economy is trying to conceptualize these issues.

We must add the consideration that for small countries, the political cycle leads to extreme instability of their monetary regimes, which become hostage to the political struggle, and most often leads to inflation, devaluation and financial crisis (often referred to as "financial and inflationary trauma"). That is, in small countries, the dependence of the monetary regime on domestic factors is relatively greater and more harmful than their external dependence (that of the external monetary centres). The history of monetary regimes in the Balkans shows this.

Finally, in addition to monetary regimes, dependence can also occur in informal monetary practices that are also part of a country's monetary system. The most common form is that of *"currency substitution"*. It is expressed in the preferences of the economic agents of the small and peripheral country to pay, measure and save in a stable foreign currency, chosen by consumers and producers.

Basically, these processes are dictated by the rate of inflation and the depreciation of the exchange rate. The fact is that Balkan countries are an area with a strong currency substitution, which is closely monitored and regularly studied (i.e. by the Austrian Central Bank).[32] Currency substitution can be observed both in the official sector—in the balance sheets of banks (loans and deposits in foreign currency) and in the informal (undeclared) economy. In the grey sector, in general, payments in foreign banknotes and in large denominations are extremely common. These substitution processes further shrink the fiscal base (as well as the sources of seigniorage) of the peripheral countries, which, as we have pointed out, are forced to comply with a conservative financial policy.

[30] For a discussion on coalitions among internal and external actors, see Chapter 3.

[31] See, for example, Abdelal (2005), Feldmann (2013), Schobert (2003).

[32] See also ECB, Windischbauer (2016).

As an appendage, we will recall that in the synopsis of monetary hierarchy within the monetary pyramid, B. Cohen lists the following types of national money (in an order of increasing dependence and abandonment of monetary sovereignty)—(i) top currency, (ii) patrician currency, (iii) elite currency, (iv) plebeian currency (v) permeated currency, (vi) quasi currency and (vii) pseudo currency (Cohen, 1998, 113–118, and Cohen, 2015, 15–19). In our opinion, Balkan currencies, with very few exceptions (and in certain periods), represent the last three types of currency (permeated currency, quasi currency and pseudo currency[33]).

As a whole, (formal or informal) monetary hierarchy and monetary dependency cannot be eradicated. It needs to be managed successfully. Strong and weak currencies have always existed in history (Asselain & Plessis, 2003). From a historical perspective, this hierarchical nature has always existed, either within the colonial monetary systems, or the international monetary system—i.e. between individual colonial monetary systems and other areas. The historical dependence and hierarchical subordination of monetary regimes in the Balkan countries have also been a well-documented fact since the time of the Latin Monetary Union (Einaudi, 2008; Nenovsky & Vaslin, 2020).

In Chapters 6 and 7, we will present illustrations of the presented theoretical constructs, focusing on the modern dependent regimes on the Balkans (Currency boards and euroization). But beforehand, it is necessary to show how dependent capitalism has gradually emerged in the new EU member states during the 1990s and 2000s.

References

Abdelal, R. (2005). *National purpose in the world economy: Post-soviet states in comparative perspective*. Cornell University Press.

Aglietta, M., & Orléan, A. (1982). *La violence de la monnaie*. PUF.

Amable, B. (2003). *The diversity of modern capitalism*. Oxford University Press.

Aoki, M. (1994). The contingent governance of teams: Analysis of institutional complementarity. *International Economic Review, 35*(3), 657–676.

Asselain, J.-Ch., & Plessis, A. (2003). Banques centrales, monnaies fortes et monnaies faibles de la fin du XIX siècle à la Seconde Guerre mondiale. In O. Feiertag & M. Margairaz (Eds.), *Politiques et pratiques des banques d'émission en Europe (XVIIe-XXe siècle)* (pp. 257–298). Albin Michel.

[33] We will also note a number of new studies regarding the monetary pyramid from the positions of the Modern Monetary Theory (Bonizzi et al., 2019).

Balino, T., & Enoch, C. (Eds.). (1997). *Currency board arrangements: Issues and experiences* (IMF Occasional Paper No. 151). International Monetary Fund.

Bonizzi, B., Kaltenbrunner, A., & Michell, J. (2019). Monetary sovereignty is a spectrum: Modern monetary theory and developing countries. *Real-World Economics Review, 89*, 46–61.

Camillieri Gilson, M-T. (2002). *Policy pre-commitment and institutional design: A synthetic indicator applied to currency boards* (OECD working paper No. 16).

Coats, W. (2007). *One currency for Bosnia*. Ottawa, Jameson Books Inc.

Cohen, B. (2015). *Currency power*. Princeton University Press.

Cohen, B. (1998). *The geography of money*. Cornel University Press.

de Bernis, G., & Bye, M. (1987). *Relations économiques internationales*. Daloz.

Desquilbet, J.-B., & Nenovsky, N. (2004). Credibility and adjustment: Gold Standards and Currency Boards Compared, *William Davidson Institute WP* N° 692.

Dixon-Fyle, S. (1978). Monetary dependence in Africa: The case of Sierra Leone. *The Journal of Modern African Studies, 16*(2), 273–294.

Drahokoupil, J., & Myant, M. (2011). *Transition economies: Political economy in Russia, Eastern Europe, and Central Asia*. John Wiley & Sons.

Einaudi, L. (2008). Monetary separation and the European convergence in the Balkans in the 19th century. In *The experience of exchange rate regimes in South-Eastern Europe in a historical and comparative perspective* (pp. 30–49). Oesterreichische Nationalbank.

Edwards, S. (2020). *Milton Friedman and exchange rates in developing countries* (NBER Working Paper No. 27975)

Fabris, N., Vukajlovic-Grba, D., Radunović, T., & Janković H. H. (2004). *Economic policy in dollarized economies with a special review of montenegro* (WP N°1). The Central Bank of Montenegro.

Feldmann, M. (2013). From the Ruble Zone to the Euro zone: The political economy of Estonian Macroeconomic policy. *Post-Soviet Affairs, 29*(4), 354–370.

Fischer, S. (1982). Seigniorage and the case for a national money. *Journal of Political Economy, 90*(2), 295–313.

Fischer, S. (2001). Exchange rate regimes: Is the bipolar view correct?, *Journal of Economic Perspectives, 15*(2), 3–24.

Friedman, M. (1973). *Money and economic development: The Horowitz lectures of 1972*. Praeger Publishers.

Hanke, S. (2002a). Currency boards. *Annals of the American academy of Political and Social Science, 579*, 87–105.

Hanke, S. (2002b). On dollarization and currency boards: Error and deception. *Policy Reform, 5*(4), 203–222.

Heilperin, M. (1939). *International monetary economics, Longmans*. Green and Co.

Helleiner, E. (2003). *The making of national money: Territorial currencies in historical perspective*. Cornell University Press.

Gedeon, S. (2013). Stability properties of the currency board: Case study of Bosnia and Herzegovina 2004–2010. *Bank and Bank Systems, 8*(3), 87–99.

Gerschenkroon, A. (1962). *Economic backwardness in historical perspective*. Harvard University Press.

Guilaumont-Jeanneney, S. (2015). *Régimes et stratégies de change dans les pays en développement*. Economica.

Grittersovà, J. (2014). Exchange rates in transition economies. In Th. Oatley (Ed.), The *International political economy of the international monetary and financial system*. Edward Elgar

International Monetary Fund. (2020). *Annual report on exchange arrangements and exchange restrictions 2019*. IMF.

Kydland, F., & Wynne, M. (2002). Alternative monetary constitutions and the quest for price stability. *Federal Reserve Bank of Dallas Economic and Financial Policy Review, 1*(1), 1–19.

Le Vuolo, R., & Pereira, J. M. (2018). De la pérdida de soberanía monetaria a la pérdida de soberanía política: Los ejemplos de Argentina y Grecia, *Documentos de Trabajo CIEPP N° 101*, Centro Interdisciplinario para el Estudio de Políticas Públicas.

Magnin. (2020). Diversity of capitalism in the New EU Member States. In A. Farazmand (Ed.), *Global encyclopaedia of public administration, public policy, and governance*, Springer, Cham

Magnin, E., & Nenovsky, N. (2021). Dependent monetary regimes in the Balkans: Enlarging the "varieties of capitalism" hypothesis. *International Journal of Public Administration, 44*(14), 1216–1230.

Magnin, E., & Nenovsky, N. (2022). Balkan monetary dependence during the XIXth and XXth centuries. *Economic Alternatives*, (2), 171–200.

Marinova, T., & Nenovsky, N. (2019). Towards understanding Balkan economic thought: Preliminary reflections. *History of Economic Thought and Policy, 1*, 29–50.

Mehrling, P. (2015). Elasticity and discipline in the global swap network. *International Journal of Political Economy, 44*, 311–324.

Mongelli, P. (2002). "New" views on the optimum currency area theory: What is EMU telling us? *ECB WP*, No. 138.

Nenovsky, N., & Vaslin, J. M. (2020). Shadowing the Latin monetary union: Monetary regimes and interest rates at the Balkans Periphery (1867–1912). *The Journal of European Economic History, 23*(2), 71–114.

Nenovsky, N., & Penchev, P. (2015). Reconstructing eclecticism: Bulgarian economic thought in the Ottoman empire in the 19th century. *History of Political Economy, 47*(4), 631–664.
Nenovsky, N., & Chobanov, P. (2020). Les limites su seignoriage au Liban, *Commerce du Lavant*, Octobre, online
Nenovsky, N., & Mihaylova Borisova, G. (2015). Debts, ideas and interests in the Balkans: Chronology of the post-communist transformation, 1990–2013, *Economie et Institutions, 23*(2), 121–145
Nenovsky, N., Tochkov, K., & Turcu, C. (2013). Monetary regime and eu accession: Comparing Bulgaria and Romania. *Communist and Post-Communist Studies, 46*(1), 13–23.
Nenovsky, N., & Villieu, P. (2011). EU enlargement and monetary regimes from the insurance model perspectives. *Post-Communist Economies, 23*(4), 433–447.
Nenovsky, N. (2009). *Monetary regimes in post-communist countries: Some long-term reflections* (Working Paper No. 2). Agency for Economic Analysis and Forecasting.
Nenovsky, N. (2007). *Monetary order: Critic of monetary theory* (Siela, Sofia, Ed.) (in Bulgarian)
Nenovsky, N., & Rizopoulos, Y. (2003). Extreme monetary regime change. evidence from the currency board introduction in Bulgaria. *Journal of Economic Issues, 37*(4), 909–941.
Nenovsky, N., Hristov, K., & Mihaylov, M. (2001). Comparing currency board automatic mechanism in Bulgaria, Estonia and Lithuania. *Journal des Economistes et des Etudes Humaines, 11*(4), 575–616.
North, D. (1990a). Institutions and Their consequences for the economic performance. In K. Cook & M. Levi (Eds.), *The limits of rationality* (pp. 383–401). University of Chicago Press.
North, D. (1990b). *Institutions, institutional change and economic performance.* Cambridge University Press.
Schobert, F. (2003). *Die unilaterale Einführungeiner Fremdwährung. Währungswahl, Seigniorage und Zinsprämieneffekte in mittel- undosteuropäischen Ländern*, Schriftenreihe volkswirtschaftliche Forschungsergebnisse, Verlag Dr. Kovac.
Schuler, K. (1999). The problem with pegged exchange rates. *Kyklos, 52*(1), 83–102.
Schwartz, A. (1993). Currency boards: Their past, present, and possible future role. *Carnegie-Rochester Conference Series on Public Policy, 39*, 147–187.
Simmons, B. (1996). Rulers of the game: Central bank independence during the interwar years. *International Organization, 50*(3), 407–443.

Thirlwall, A. (2011 [1979]). The balance of payments constraint as an explanation of the international growth rate differences. *PSL Quarterly Review, 64*(259), 429–438.

White, L. (2020, June 19). *Should the U.S. government create a token-based digital dollar?* CATO Institute.

Windischbauer, U. (2016). *Strengthening the role of local currencies in EU candidate and potential candidate countries* (ECB Occasional Paper No. 170).

Zimmermann, C. (2013). The concept of monetary sovereignty revisited. *The European Journal of International Law, 24*(3), 797–818.

PART II

Empirical and Historical Perspectives

CHAPTER 5

Dependent Capitalism in Central and Eastern Europe

Abstract The purpose of this chapter is to show how initial conditions in 1989–1990, the legacy of the former socialist system, and both processes of transition and integration into the EU, marked by exceptional institutional reforms, have led to the emergence of a model of dependent capitalism in Central and Eastern Europe in the 2000s. While this model is unique at a certain level of abstraction, it nevertheless presents differentiated variants associated with the forms of dependencies that characterize it. The 2008 economic and financial crisis highlighted the fragilities of dependent capitalism and of its institutional variations. The post-socialist capitalism has nevertheless retained its main institutional features after the crisis, in particular its dependence on foreign direct investment. However, in recent years, some countries seem to be reconsidering this model and giving a more important role to the national State.

Keywords Perceived legacy · Path dependence · Washington consensus · Shock therapy · Financial dependence · Remittances · Dependence on FDI and exports

E. Magnin and N. Nenovsky, *Diversity of Capitalism in Central and Eastern Europe*, https://doi.org/10.1007/978-3-031-04950-7_5

Introduction

History matters. The emergence of dependent capitalism in Central and Eastern Europe is the result of a historical process of exceptional institutional change, that began in the early 1990s, and which is marked by the former socialist system's legacy. The latter is not the only explanatory factor; national elite strategies and the influence of external forces, the European Union, international organizations (IMF, World Bank...) and multinational firms, have also played a decisive role. But historical legacy remains an important element in interaction with these other factors. In that sense, CEE dependent capitalism is also «path dependent». Defined in simple terms, the concept of path dependence refers to the idea that the outcome of a process of change that unfolds over time is difficult to predict because it depends on the path taken (Arthur, 1990; David, 1985). Several trajectories are possible without it being possible to predict a priori which one will be selected. Any prediction is therefore impossible and only an ex-post analysis allows us to understand the outcome of the process. But on the other hand, the lock-in possibility and the reduction in the space of choices implied by the concept of path dependence increase the probability of future scenarios and make it possible to carry out an ex ante analysis (North, 1990). The concept's originality thus lies in blurring the boundaries between determinism and indeterminism. This concept has been successfully applied to institutional change in general and to post-socialist transformation in particular (Chavance & Magnin, 2002; Magnin, 2002; Stark, 1992).

In this perspective, Bohle and Greskovits (2012) propose the concept of "perceived inheritance". It is not the legacy per se that ultimately matters, but the way in which the main economic and political actors perceive this heritage, the complexity of which allows for different interpretations. The impact on reform strategies will be different depending on whether it is perceived negatively or positively. The perceived legacy and the liberal-inspired reforms undertaken in the various countries have led to the emergence of a dependent capitalism in the 2000s (presented in Chapter 3), whose fragilities have been revealed through the 2008 financial crisis. Despite the difficulties encountered in most of the NMS (New Member States), albeit mitigated in Poland, the Czech Republic and Slovakia, post-socialist capitalism has maintained its main institutional features since, in particular its dependence on foreign direct investment.

Perceived Legacy and Path Dependence in Shaping National Transformation Trajectories (1989–1998)

Building on Bohle and Greskovits' work, three types of perceived legacy can be distinguished here: the positively perceived legacy of the Visegrád countries (and Slovenia), the negatively perceived legacy of the Baltic countries and the legacy perceived as a factor of stability in Southeast Europe. In addition to the perceived legacy, there are «objective» macroeconomic initial conditions, such as debt, inflation, savings, likely to play a significant role in the choice of reforms.

The Impact of a Positively Perceived Legacy in East-Central Europe

The Visegrád countries did not reject the socialist period's legacy as a whole. On the contrary, at the beginning of the 1990s, they sought to reconcile some past "institutional achievements" with the neo-liberal reforms promoted by international organizations and summarized in the Washington Consensus (Lipton & Sachs, 1990a, b; Williamson, 1990; World Bank, 1996).[1]

In *Hungary*, the waves of reforms carried out since 1968 allowed the country to durably move away from the Soviet model, so that in the 1980s, it benefited from a partly liberated, west-oriented economy and many institutions necessary for the functioning of a market economy (Chavance, 2019). Under these conditions, the first post-socialist Hungarian government opted for a gradualist transformation strategy in the first half of the 1990s, more in line with the Hungarian socio-political compromise inherited from the Kadar era (Kornai, 1996). However, the foreign debt burden, also a legacy of Kadarism, strongly constrained the government's privatization strategy, which gave priority to assets sales to foreign investors. This strategy has paid off, as evidenced by the significant flow of foreign direct investment (FDI) to Hungary (Fig. 5.1). Proximity to Western European markets and a reputation for openness to the West have helped build the trust needed. The exceptional willingness to honour the debt without renegotiation has undoubtedly reinforced this trend, supported if necessary by an advantageous tax

[1] Slovenia will not be mentioned here. Nevertheless, it belongs to the group of countries that consider positively some aspects of their socialist legacy, especially the participation of social partners in economic decisions.

policy. The country's inherited infrastructure and skilled labour force also influenced the FDI destination choice. In return, the large amount of FDI has helped the country to repay part of its debt. In addition, these capital flows have contributed to modernize the productive apparatus and boost exports. Maintaining a form of "state paternalism" towards firms and households is also part of the Kadarist legacy and the search for a stable socio-economic compromise after 1990 (Kornai 1980, 1996). For the former, it involves financial aid and state interventions with banks to facilitate access to credit. For the latter, it is a question of preserving a welfare system, inherited from the socialist and pre-socialist periods (Wagener, 2002). However, state paternalism contributed to macroeconomic instability. Not without debate, the new government that came to power in 1994 adopted a new stabilization program the following year (the Bokros Plan), which marked a change in Hungary's trajectory, with the start of a welfare reform and an acceleration of privatization, in the context of an application for the opening of EU pre-accession negotiations.

Poland has also benefited from the reforms carried out during the socialist period, which brought Polish institutions closer to those of a market economy. However, unlike its Magyar neighbour, these reforms were accompanied by violent social conflicts (which led, among other things, to the creation of the independent trade union *Solidarność* in 1980). Economic reforms and recurrent social conflicts gradually destabilized the Polish economic and political systems. In 1989, the Polish economy had to face hyperinflation, which convinced the post-socialist government to adopt a shock therapy policy (Köves, 1992). Similarly, the high Polish debt burden at the end of the Socialist period will not have the same effect on the transformation trajectory. Unlike Hungary, Poland decided to renegotiate its debt with her creditors, which makes the choice of a privatization strategy centred on direct sales to foreign investors less compelling, all the more so since the latter were reluctant to invest in an unstable Poland that was not inclined to repay its debts. Privatization methods have been quite diverse and resulted in a relative diversity of forms of ownership and corporate control. Employee buy-outs have been very successful, institutionalizing in broad daylight the informal property rights acquired by workers in their struggle against power in the 1980s. As a result, privatization proceeded slowly and the Polish economy in the 1990s was not yet a host country for FDI and was not yet integrated into European production networks. Under these conditions, state intervention remained very active until the end of the 1990s to support large state-owned enterprises and banks restructuring and to mitigate the transition's social costs by maintaining a relatively generous and inherited from the past welfare system.

Unlike Hungary and Poland, the former Czechoslovakia remained committed to the centralized model until 1989. The 1968 "Prague Spring" put an end to any attempt at reform. Nevertheless, the country inherited a rather favourable macroeconomic situation from this period, which gave it more freedom than its reformist neighbours to choose its transformation strategy. After the "Velvet Revolution", the Czech-Slovak divorce, implemented on January 1, 1993, also proceeded smoothly. The new *Czech Republic* continued the strategy of liberal transformation begun in 1991. The choice of a shock therapy was surprising, given the country's macroeconomic stability. Beyond the liberal rhetoric which V. Klaus used skilfully, especially when it came to sending a signal to international organizations about his government's unfailing reformist will, the challenge was to initiate a rapid and radical transformation of the economic system, which had been made possible by an uncompromising political transition and by agents who had not experienced reform. Mass privatization met this challenge and demonstrated a sensitivity to initial conditions. It opened the possibility of creating a "popular" capitalism, in a context where the lack of savings might leave ownership in the hands of former nomenklaturists or foreign investors. Under these conditions, only national (state-owned) banks were able to buy up firms in the mass privatization process, giving rise to a hybrid form of "interwoven ownership" (Chavance & Magnin, 2002; Mertlik, 1997; Stark, 1996). The Czech transition in the first half of the 1990s was not so liberal eventually. «State paternalism» was still very present to protect Czech industrial "flagships" and households. This policy resulted in the absence of large-scale companies' bankruptcies and in keeping unprofitable companies in business with the help of state-supported bank credit. On the household side, the low unemployment rate, the preservation of a decent level of social protection, and the control of some «sensitive» product prices made it possible to implement reforms with a fairly broad social consensus. However, the perverse effects generated by the Czech model, notably low competitiveness and the accumulation of non-performing loans in banks' balance sheets, led to a serious economic and financial crisis in 1997. The government was then forced to adopt a new stabilization program and to take measures to strengthen companies' and banks' financial discipline.

After the split of Czechoslovakia, *Slovakia*, under the leadership of Prime Minister Vladimír Mečiar, chose a different path from that of the Czech Republic. The new leader followed the line of former president Gustáv Husák who, after 1968, made the economic catching-up of Slovak lands a priority (Bohle & Greskovits, 2012). He revived state paternalism, protective of businesses and households, with a touch of nationalism, in an attempt to foster the emergence of a Slovak capitalism. He cancelled the mass privatization program and favoured a model based on selling companies to Slovak "managers", preferably loyal to the government. He pursued a policy of developing national infrastructures and restructuring large industrial enterprises, financed by state banks. Regardless of the country's macroeconomic records, the Mečiar regime's authoritarian style would not allow Slovakia to qualify for the first wave of EU accession negotiations, a refusal that would be felt as a cruel humiliation and would contribute to undermine Mečiar's government's legitimacy and to its downfall in 1998.

Reforms Rejecting Socialist Legacy in the Baltic Countries

In the Baltic countries, unlike the countries of Central-Eastern Europe, the legacy of the former socialist system is perceived negatively (Bohle & Greskovits, 2012). This rejection is linked to the memory of the USSR's annexation of their territories in 1940 and the forced sovietization that followed. It is reflected in a will to break with the past and affirm the country's regained independence. The break is confirmed with the implementation, at the beginning of the 1990s, of some of the most radical stabilization and transition programs, first by Estonia, followed by Latvia and, to a lesser extent, Lithuania. Beyond their similarities, the national trajectories appear relatively differentiated, due to specific initial conditions and political paths of extrication. The exclusion of the Russian-speaking minorities from political life at the beginning of the 1990s in Estonia and Latvia influenced the structuring of political representation in the sense of a less left/right polarization with an increased personalization around strong competing personalities. In Lithuania, where the population is more homogeneous, debates on reforms were more intense between opposing camps, leading to a more gradual transition process.

In Estonia, the radical break and independence from the former USSR combined with the restoration of the national currency and the creation of a Currency board as early as 1992, even before the IMF adopted it, strictly pegging the Estonian kroon to the German mark and severely constraining monetary policy (see Chapter 6 on Currency boards). For the Estonian government, the Currency board made it possible to isolate monetary creation from political interference, which was common in the former system. Moreover, the currency's stability was a source of national pride, while the elites no longer hesitated to draw a parallel with the interwar period and the introduction of the gold standard. In Latvia, the very restrictive monetary policy implemented, combined with the creation of a new currency (in two stages: Latvian rouble and then lats), actually played a very close role to that of a Currency board. The 1920s and 1930s also appeared to be one of the inspiration sources for Latvian monetary policy. In Lithuania, a Currency board was not adopted until 1994, after intense debate and with IMF support.

Estonian radical and neo-liberal reformism, expressing the desire to break with the past, were also reflected in a series of institutional changes aimed at a greater economic liberalization: full foreign trade opening, adoption of a flat tax regime as early as 1994 and residual welfare policy. Lithuania also introduced a flat tax system in 1994 and Latvia in 1997. This tax regime, like the Currency board, offered the advantage of simplicity and did not require a high level of administrative skills that were lacking after socialist time (Magnin, 2009). "Rejecting" the legacy of a relatively generous welfare system, the Baltic governments decided to keep reducing its size, especially since its financing appeared to be a problem in a context where the Currency board on the one hand and the tax regime on the other strongly constrained monetary and fiscal policies. In the same way, the will to break with the past and the budgetary constraints encouraged Baltic governments to put an end to state paternalism towards companies, by favouring privatization by direct sale to foreign investors in Estonia and Latvia and/or by refusing any form of industrial policy.[2] It would result in a sharp industrial decline compared to the Visegrád countries.

In 1997, Estonia, unlike its two neighbours, was among the lucky ones selected to start EU accession negotiations. This success was due

[2] The choice of the privatization method is also dictated by Estonian and Latvian governments' will not to favour former company directors and Russian-speaking workers. Lithuania, having no such concerns, implemented a mass privatization program between 1991 and 1995. Foreign direct investment will remain low during the period compared to other Baltic countries.

not only to Scandinavian countries' support, but also to its image as a model country, of a successful transition to a market economy, strengthened by its macroeconomic results, which brought it recognition from international organizations. However, its integration into international trade is less favourable than the one of Central and Eastern European countries. Latvia and Lithuania, for their part, will have to wait until the following decade to win their "Baltic tigers" label. In any case, the three countries' economic development is still very dependent on trade relations with Russia, especially Latvia, which contrasts with the desire for a radical break with the past.

Bulgaria and Romania Hold on to the Past

In 1990, Bulgaria and Romania started their transition process with tougher initial conditions. This binding legacy would significantly shape their national trajectories, probably more than elsewhere in Eastern Europe (Magnin, 2002). It paradoxically appeared to be a stabilizing factor in a context of great uncertainty.

Poorer and remote from Western European markets, both South-Eastern European countries inherited from the planned economy a more difficult productive structure to adapt to global demand, in which agriculture played an important role. Moreover, Bulgaria remained highly dependent on trade with the former USSR; its dissolution, and that of the CMEA (Council for Mutual Economic Assistance), hit the country severely. On the eve of transition, both countries also suffered from serious macroeconomic imbalances. Bulgaria and Romania borrowed massively from abroad under the communist regime, but while the former inherited a high external debt in 1990, the latter chose to rapidly repay its creditors during the 1980s at the cost of a drastic reduction in imports, which accentuated its autarkic tendencies, and harsh sacrifices imposed on the population. To further darken the picture, these countries were ruled by very authoritarian regimes, reluctant to follow the wind of reform that blew in the 1980s in Eastern Europe. Under these conditions, it was not surprising that the economic and political exits from the socialist system were painful and sometimes violent.

The Bulgarian and Romanian post-socialist trajectories shared some similarities in the first half of the 1990s. In both countries, elite continuity was significant. The first post-socialist governments were ruled by "neo-communist" parties, emanations of the former communist party.

Under these conditions, inherited informal institutions tend to persist, including a form of clientelism related to the former elite's networks. Structural reforms were progressing slowly in this context, especially since the binding legacy did not facilitate the transition and people were suspicious about markets in countries that were not reform-oriented until then. Moreover, trade unions and workers remained mobilized and did not hesitate to make their voices heard, especially the Jiu Valley miners. Large state-owned enterprises were being privatized slowly in both countries and foreign direct investment remained very low. State paternalism towards households and enterprises hampered any willingness to restructuring and maintained a relatively soft budget constraint (Kornai, 1980). Nevertheless, it is worth mentioning the "progress" made during the first half of the 1990s, which contributed to growth return in 1994–1995: adaptation of the legislative framework to a market economy, creation of small private enterprises, usually in trade and services, and reorientation of foreign trade towards Western European countries.

However, large state-owned enterprises have been able to avoid a painful adjustment and maintain their activities while accumulating losses, thanks to state support (subsidies, low-rate credits, debt relief, and swelling arrears to the state, the banking sector, and sometimes to employees). As a result, large state-owned banks recorded an impressive increase in non-performing loans in their portfolios, compelling the Bulgarian and Romanian governments to refinance them, worsening fiscal problems in a context of low tax discipline (inherited from the former system) and inflationary pressures. In 1996, a serious financial and political crisis brought Bulgaria to the brink of chaos (see Chapter 6 for more details); Romania barely avoided it. In both countries, a government change and international organizations intervention led to the adoption of a "shock therapy" type stabilization program and the acceleration of structural reforms (UNECE, 1997, 1999).

Emergence of a Dependent Capitalism with Various Forms in the 2000s and Its Resilience to the 2008 Crisis

The ambiguous results of liberal reforms in an underestimated inherited institutional context (EBRD, 1999; Magnin, 1999; Portes, 1993; Stiglitz, 1999; UNECE, 1992, 1997, 1999; World Bank, 2002, 2005) paradoxically prompt most Eastern European governments to move faster and further along the path of privatizing the remaining state-owned firms and banks, of liberalizing the economy and opening it up to foreign capital. The effects of early 1990s reforms are thus partly constraining the next stages of the transformation process. The liberal temptation is all the stronger as the EU accession process is underway and implies a convergence of candidate countries to "the" European model. Surprisingly, the EU does not promote its social model and, on the contrary, urges CEE countries to adopt reforms and, eventually, a more liberal model than in the EU-15: higher flexibility of the labour market, downsizing welfare reforms (retirement, health, education), flat tax regimes, public utilities privatization, etc. This program became widespread throughout the zone.

Persistent inherited problems, the lack of capital and skills and in some cases a high external debt also appear decisive in the choice of opening the economy to foreign investors. The stable horizon set by EU membership in turn strengthens the strategy followed by reassuring the latter, which no longer hesitates to bring their capital into an institutional environment deemed more favourable. In this respect, the Visegrád countries (and Slovenia) were unquestionably the most attractive in the mid-1990s, given their geographical and institutional proximity to Western countries inherited from the former system (Fig. 5.1). They were all the more so since they included the countries selected by the EU in 1997 to be part of the first accession wave, along with Estonia, whose positive (though denied) legacy has been previously emphasized, but with the exception of Mečiar's Slovakia. During the 2000s, Baltic countries, Bulgaria and Romania, will join the first wave, catch up on their institutional "backwardness", accelerate the liberalization and privatization of the economy and in turn experience an inflow of foreign capital. These large inflows and the liberal reforms adopted in all the new EU member states lead to the emergence of a model of "dependent" capitalism with a variety of national forms (identified by Nölke and Vliegenthart [2009] and Drahokoupil and Myant [2011]). As mentioned in Chapter 3, it is possible to make a distinction between: a form of dependence on FDI combined with a strong dependence on exports to Western Europe, a form of financial dependence related to external credit inflows, and a dependence on workers' remittances and international aid. These various forms of dependence do not allow a clear dividing line to be drawn between countries. On the contrary, they are likely to be combined together, with each country having a different configuration depending on the extent of each form of dependence.

Dependence on FDI and Exports

Several countries exhibit a first form of dependence on foreign capital and exports, mostly to the EU. As early as the 1990s, they experienced a significant inflow of FDI, which, cumulatively, represent in the 2000s and 2010s a significant share in GDP (Fig. 5.1). The share of exports in GDP is well above EU-27 average and the share of exports to other EU countries is also very high (Fig. 5.2). These concerns primarily the small East-Central European countries, whose growth is driven by the development of exports, which is itself sustained by foreign investment. Hungary, the Czech Republic and Slovakia best illustrate this form of dependence, to which Estonia, Poland and Slovenia can also be associated, with some qualifications (discussed below).

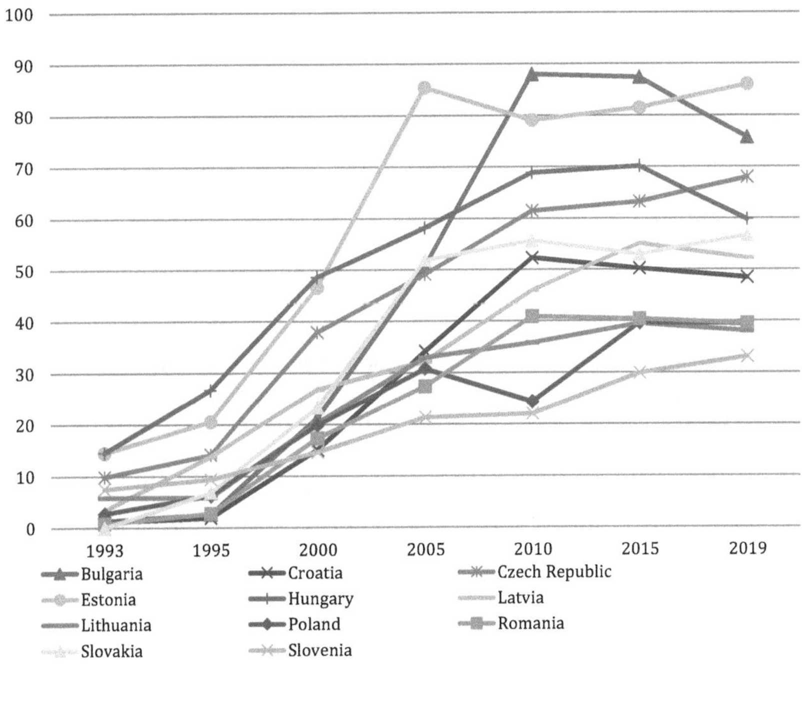

Fig. 5.1 FDI inward stock in EU new member states (% of GDP, 1993–2019) (*Source* WIIW FDI Report [various years])

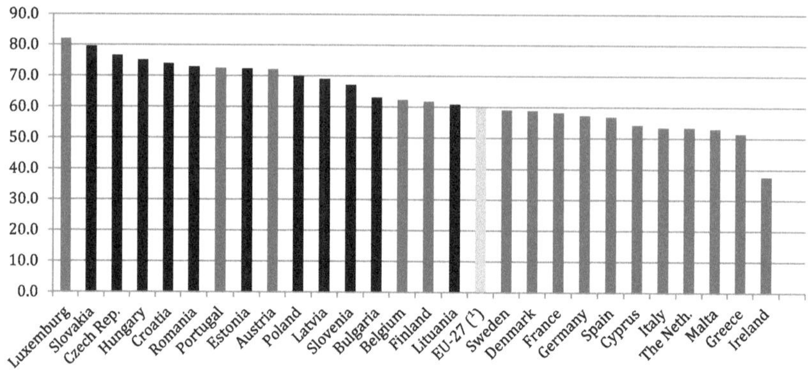

Fig. 5.2 Intra-EU-27 trade in goods, 2019 (IM + EX, % of total trade) ([1] Weighted average. NMS in black. *Source* Eurostat)

These countries benefited from an initial advantage related to the (deemed) favourable organizational and institutional legacy from the socialist system. Industrial development during the communist period, with a specialization for some countries in transport equipment, machine tools and electrical equipment may have influenced the choice of investors. However, as the productive configurations were relatively similar in Eastern Europe, investors' preference for Central Europe during the 1990s can be explained above all by the institutional reforms carried out before the Wall fell and a rapid convergence towards Western economies afterwards (Chavance & Magnin, 2000). The selection of these countries (with the exception of Slovakia) in the first wave of countries selected for accession contributed to reinforcing their political and economic stability and attracting investors. During the 2000s, this initial advantage turned into a cumulative process, with the accumulation of capital leading to industrial structure modernization, skills and competitiveness improvement, thus attracting even more capital, especially from competitors and suppliers willing to follow their customers, eventually leading to the formation of industrial clusters in the region, notably in the automotive industry. As competition between FDI host countries was growing, Central European governments did not hesitate to offer multinational firms generous subsidies and attractive taxation, engaging in a tax and social competition that proved disastrous for their public finances (Magnin, 2009).

In East-Central Europe, foreign capital has been flowing into the so-called "complex" industrial sectors, which are more technology-and labour-intensive, sustaining the development of exports in these very sectors. If this type of integration into international trade holds a potential for bringing productive systems closer to Western European economies, the degree of "complexity" of these systems remains dependent on foreign firms and their contributions in capital, innovation and skills.

No country perfectly matches the aforementioned dependence model. As the sole big country of the group, Poland's export weight (about 55% in 2019, Eurostat) appears to be just above EU-27 average (about 49% in 2019). However, the share of intra-EU trade is much higher than EU-27 average (Fig. 5.2). Accumulated FDI inflows into the country are lower than those of other "first wave" participants, as Poland was initially reluctant to open up to foreign capital, especially in the 1990s (Fig. 5.1). This was also the case for Slovenia, which, on the other hand, shows a profile of a small and very open exporting country (exports account for about 84% of GDP in 2019) but is among the new members states closest to EU average in terms of intra-regional trade (Fig. 5.2). While Estonia fits well with the above dependence pattern, given its export weight (about 73% of GDP in 2019) and huge inflow of foreign capital (Fig. 5.1), most FDI has not been concentrated in "complex" industrial sectors, but rather in commodities and services.

The 2008 economic and financial crisis brought an end to the period of sustained growth that followed the 2004 enlargement and revealed the fragilities of dependent capitalism and its institutional variants. The countries associated with this first form of dependence had to face a decline in demand from Western Europe and a sharp contraction in capital flows. However, given the above-mentioned favourable cumulative process, partly related to the legacy of the former system, the Visegrád countries, especially Poland, the Czech Republic and Slovakia, have resisted the crisis better than most other CEE countries.[3] After a recession phase in 2009, they were able to quickly restore growth. Remarkably, Poland has not experienced a decline in GDP. It has been able to rely on its large domestic market and public investment. In general, these countries,

[3] Hungary stands out of this group because it also experiences a form of financial dependence presented in the next section.

better integrated into global value chains—especially the German ones—have been able to maintain their competitiveness and boost their exports, notably thanks to an exchange rate depreciation. The relative stability of their banking and financial sectors despite the crisis and prudent fiscal policy also had a positive impact on their economies. They also pursued their liberal-inspired welfare reforms (health, education, retirement and labour market). Transportation equipment and machine tools remain their strong sectors, but in activity segments where added value remains low (assembly in particular), which tends to leave these countries in a situation of semi-peripheral economies.

Financial Dependence

During the 2000s, Baltic countries, Bulgaria and Romania, have caught up with the Visegrád Group overcoming their institutional "backwardness" and compensated for their initial disadvantage related to a less favourable legacy, thanks to the accession process and the adoption of the *acquis communautaire* chapters. This process facilitated institutional convergence with other EU members and stabilized investors' expectations. The EU has also promoted East European economies' liberalization. In this context, FDI has flowed into these countries initially neglected by investors. But, whereas in Central Europe FDI accumulation resulted in a positive cumulative process, in the Baltic and South-Eastern European countries the path dependent and cumulative process had a less favourable effect. The lower inflow of foreign capital in the 1990s further limited the modernization of the industrial structure inherited from the socialist system. The adoption of radical liberal reforms also contributed to the increasing difficulties of industry, which was unable to cope with international competition. While clusters in "complex" industrial sectors were growing stronger in Central Europe, the other new Member states found themselves more and more behind and these very sectors were in decline. Foreign capital then found its way to other, more traditional sectors, such as light industry, resource-intensive sectors and services, which were considered all the more promising by multinational firms because they did not consider it necessary, given the size of the target market, to further develop their FDI in "complex" sectors.

FDI has thus flowed into the banking and real estate sectors, contributing to the emergence of a second form of dependent capitalism based on financial dependence and a growth regime fuelled by abundant

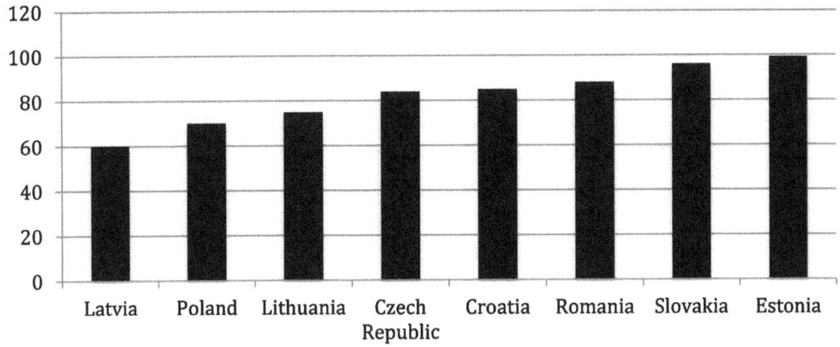

Fig. 5.3 Share of foreign banks in the banking system in selected CEE countries in the 2000s (% assets) (*Source* EBRD, Transition Report [2009])

credit. The share of foreign capital in the banking sector has been particularly high (Fig. 5.3). As a result, it made it easier to develop credit to households and businesses, particularly in euros and at very attractive interest rates (EBRD, 2009). Among the new available financial products, housing loans to households have been very successful, boosting the construction sector, supported by a favourable tax regime and pushing property prices up. The boom in housing and consumer credit, in a context of rising wages, led to a sustained growth in the 2000s, up to the 2008 crisis, in the Baltic and South-Eastern European countries, driven by domestic demand, both investment (in construction) and consumer spending. This growth improved citizens' living conditions and compensated for the weakness of welfare systems, which had been in sharp decline since the early 1990s.

Like Baltic countries, Hungary also developed a form of financial dependence, not exclusive of its dependence on FDI and exports towards the EU.[4] Credit growth resulted in an increase in foreign currency-denominated loans (especially in Swiss francs) offered by foreign-owned banks to private agents (households and companies) at favourable interest rates. Regarding Romanian development during the 2000s, it shows a gradual shift towards the variety of the Visegrad Group's dependent capitalism, with a closer profile to Poland than to Slovakia, an increase in

[4] According to Podvrsic & Schmidt (2018), Slovenia has also experienced a form of dependent financialization since the 2000s, fuelled by an increase in foreign debt.

exports and FDI in "complex" industrial sectors, especially in energy, automobiles, steel and chemicals (Ban, 2013). With the help of subsidies and tax exemptions, Romania has succeeded in attracting multinational firms. The manufacturing sector's share in the economy (about 21% of GDP in the 2000s, World Bank) actually drives it away from the less industrialized Baltic countries and Bulgaria.

The 2008 banking crisis contributed to highlight the risks of this second form of dependence (financial this time), with a global credit contraction followed by the withdrawal of capital out of Central and Eastern European countries, leading to a liquidity crisis and a currency devaluation in a floating exchange rate regime—such as the forint—worsening the situation of foreign currency borrowing agents. The most exposed countries (Hungary, Latvia, Romania) were forced to turn to (conditional) financial support from the IMF and the EU in exchange for austerity measures, further accentuating the dependent nature of their capitalist models.

In the Baltic countries, the crisis and the credit squeeze put a halt to the strong growth of the 2000s. A severe recession occurred in 2009. But following the adoption of especially tough austerity measures and the pursuit of liberal reforms, growth quickly returned—but to what a price. In all three countries, we find a relatively similar post-crisis scenario with some national specificities. Rejecting currency devaluation, crisis adjustment has been achieved by cutting wages, particularly in the public sector, and reducing welfare spending.[5] Wage reduction improved competitiveness and boosted exports. To tackle unemployment, Baltic governments adopted a policy of increased labour market flexibility. As a result, facing economic and social difficulties, many Baltic citizens chose to emigrate as a remedy to the crisis. In the hands of foreign (Scandinavian) transnational corporations (TNCs), the banking system remained stable, with subsidiaries being supported by their parent companies. In Latvia, however, the banking system experienced a serious crisis with the beginning of a banking panic, which was curbed with the help of the

[5] Among the drastic measures adopted by the Latvian government were the public sector wage cuts, which fell by an average of 26% between June 2008 and March 2010, VAT and excise tax increases, and layoffs in the education and health sectors (EBRD 2010; IMF, 2009a).

IMF and the EU. Finally, despite the crisis, the Baltic countries maintained their liberal trajectories and continued to attract FDI in the services sector and in low value-added industrial activities (Fig. 5.1).

Confronted to the crisis and the withdrawal of foreign capital, Romania had to seek financial assistance from international organizations in 2009 and implement an adjustment program. The latter involved a 25% cut in public sector wages, a 15% reduction in welfare benefits, a 5-point increase in VAT and a reform of the pension system (EBRD, 2010; IMF, 2009b). Unlike Romania, Bulgaria did not need international financial assistance, given its tight monetary policy, which was bound by a Currency board (see Chapter 6). However, a banking panic occurred in 2014 following the difficulties faced by one of the main national banks (Corporate Commercial Bank, KTB), which eventually led to its closure. Like Romania, Bulgaria suffers from some institutional weaknesses related to widespread corruption, a large informal economy, and an inefficient administration. The privatization of remaining state-owned companies (many of them in Romania) was revived after the crisis with mixed success. In response to austerity measures, rising unemployment, poverty and inequality, protest movements took place after 2010 despite the continuous erosion of trade unions, coupled with a general mistrust in the political elite.

Hungary is a special case as it is both dependent on FDI and exports (to the EU), like other members of the Visegrád Group, and dependent on finance, like the Baltic states and Southeast Europe. Like other Central-Eastern European economies, Hungary is highly integrated into global value chains, especially European ones, but the value-added content of exports remains low. Moreover, unlike other CEE countries, Hungary did not experience the 2000s pre-crisis boom period and the crisis was more severe than in other Visegrád countries, partly because of its financial dependence. Given the country's high external debt burden, double budget and current account deficits, the sharp credit squeeze as the crisis intensified in the US and Western Europe prompted Hungary to rely on (conditional) financial assistance from the IMF and the EU at the end of 2008 to meet its refinancing needs. Moreover, Hungary's high degree of external openness (about 82% in 2019) made it particularly sensitive to falling imports from the EU, its main trading partner (Fig. 5.2). The IMF agreement provided for a reduction in the budget deficit from 3.4% in 2008 to 2.5% in 2009. To this end, the government undertook to reduce public spending by targeting public sector wages (wage freeze and elimination of the 13th month), pensions and social spending (de-indexation of benefits). These measures have probably contributed to Viktor Orbán's return to power in 2010, which marked a turning point in Hungary's trajectory (Farkas, 2016). While most governments chose to further liberalize and privatize their economies after the crisis, Orbán adopted a proactive policy of state intervention into the economy: special taxes in selected foreign-dominated sectors (banking, energy, telecommunications, retail) to bail out the state budget, nationalization in sectors considered to be strategic (banking, energy, network companies), work-oriented social protection (workfare) and subsidized employment. Nevertheless, these measures have not prevented the rise in inequality[6] and poverty.

Since 2015 and the return of the PiS (*Prawo i Sprawiedliwość*) to power, Poland has also started to alter its trajectory towards greater state intervention in the economy (nationalization of banks, development of social protection) but to a lesser extent than its Hungarian neighbour.

Dependence on Remittances

Finally, there is a third form of dependence on remittances and international aid (Drahokoupil & Myant, 2011). While it mainly concerns low-income CIS countries with limited institutional development and Western Balkan countries, it also involves some of the new EU member states, such as Croatia, the Baltic countries and Romania (Fig. 5.4). It also plays a significant role in Slovakia and Bulgaria. Remittances are generally generated by the repatriation of income from diaspora economic activities and/or cross-border work in neighbouring countries. Mainly from Western Europe, they are a source of liquidity and help stimulate domestic demand in receiving countries and reduce national current account deficits.

The 2008 crisis temporarily dried up the flow of remittances from European countries affected by unemployment, such as Italy, Spain, Ireland or France. However, in most CEE countries dependent on remittances, emigration (especially of younger people) has not been stopped; on the contrary, it appeared as a solution to the crisis' problems, such

[6] The adoption of a flat income tax in 2011 played a part.

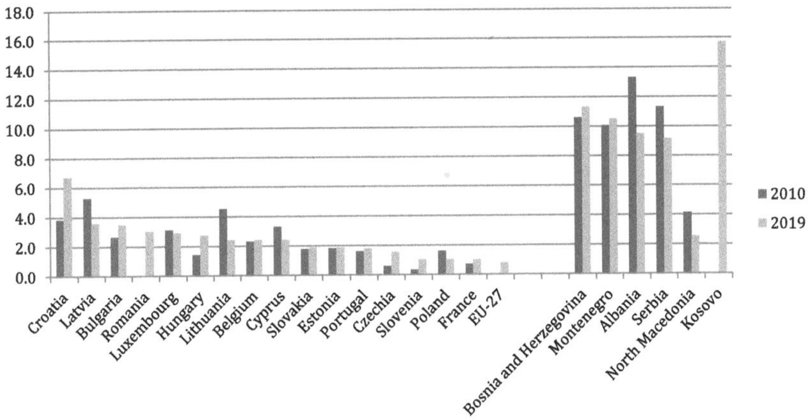

Fig. 5.4 Inbound personal remittances in the EU and Western Balkans (% of GDP $\geq$ 1 in 2019) (*Note* Missing data if not available. *Source* UNCTAD except Kosovo [Eurostat])

as rising unemployment and poverty, low wages and sometimes rejection of the political elite. Unfortunately, while it has helped to alleviate some of the negative effects of the crisis and to limit the increase in unemployment in the CEECs, emigration nevertheless remains a threat to the pension system in countries with an ageing population and more generally to the economic dynamism of these countries.

Conclusion

The emergence of a dependent capitalism in Central and Eastern Europe is the result of a historical process of transformation, marked by different initial national conditions, legacies of the socialist period, which influenced the choice of reforms adopted in the 1990s, the consequences of which in turn reduced the range of alternatives in the 2000s. As such, dependent capitalism is also "path dependent". However, it would be wrong to interpret it as a deterministic process because it is indeed the interplay of actors (political and economic leaders, TNC, international organizations, etc.), of conflicts and coalitions of interests, as well as their expectations, that shape national trajectories. This political game is nevertheless played in a specific historical institutional context, which is changing as a result of these actors' games, under the action of endogenous and exogenous forces.

If dependent capitalism appears unique at a relatively high level of abstraction, it nevertheless presents distinctive national variations, according to the forms of dependence (on foreign capital) that characterize it. Three ideal–typical forms of dependent capitalism emerged in the CEECs during the 2000s, dominated by FDIs and/or finance and/or migrant remittances, whose fragilities have been revealed by the 2008 crisis. The macroeconomic consequences of the crisis differed from one country to another, but nevertheless, dependent capitalism proved to be resilient to the crisis and preserved its main institutional characteristics (FDI, cheap and skilled labour, labour market flexibility, liberal tax regime and limited social protection…), which once again demonstrates the strength of their complementarity. However, this stability, which makes the concept of a "model" of capitalism relevant, could become locked into a low-road trajectory, marked by a specialization in low value-added activities, leaving these countries in a position of semi-peripheral economies for years (Fig. 5.5). This gloomy prospect is more likely for the Balkan countries than for East-Central Europe, given their specific historical trajectories, as the next chapters will explain.

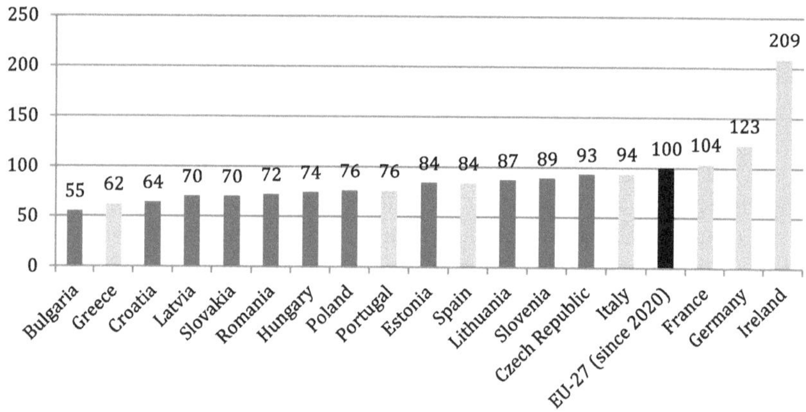

Fig. 5.5 Catching-up? GDP per capita in PPS in the NMS and selected EU countries in 2020 (Index—EU-27 = 100) (*Source* Eurostat. Ireland's success must be qualified following a change in the GDP calculation in 2015)

Since 2010, Hungary—and later Poland—have tried to change their path on their own, often in opposition to the rest of the EU, rather than promoting a collective EU economic response, favouring an upgrading of Eastern European economies by investing in research, innovation and higher education. This inflection of the Hungarian (and, to a lesser extent, Polish) trajectories could reflect a willingness to move out of dependence and could result in a shift towards state capitalism or simply mean the return to a kind of state paternalism, which has been at the heart of Hungary's socio-economic compromise since 1956.

References

Arthur, B. (1990, February). Positive feedbacks in the economy. *Scientific American, 262*(2).

Ban, C. (2013, December). *From Cocktail to dependence: Revisiting the foundations of dependent market economies* (GEGI Working Paper, no. 3).

Berend, I. (1996). *Central and Eastern Europe, 1944–1993.* Cambridge University Press.

Bohle, D., & Greskovits, B. (2012). *Capitalist diversity on Europe's periphery.* Cornell University Press.

Boyer, R. (1995). The great transformation of Eastern Europe: A "regulationist" perspective. *Emergo Journal of Transforming Economies and Societies, 2*(4), 25–41.

Chavance, B. (2019). *The transformation of communist systems: Economic reform since the 1950s.* Routledge.

Chavance, B., & Magnin, E. (2000). National trajectories of post-socialist transformation: Is there a convergence towards western capitalisms ? In M. Dobry (Ed.), *Democratic and capitalist transitions in eastern Europe: Lessons for the social sciences* (pp. 221–233). Kluwer Academic Publishers.

Chavance, B., & Magnin, E. (2002). Emergence of path-dependent mixed economies in Central Europe. In G. Hodgson (Ed.), *A modern reader in institutional and evolutionary economics: Key concepts* (pp. 168–200). Edward Elgar.

David, P. (1985). Clio and the economics of QWERTY. *American Economic Review, 75*(2).

Drahokoupil, J., & Myant, M. (2011). *Transition economies: Political economy in Russia, Eastern Europe, and Central Asia.* John Wiley & Sons.

EBRD. (1999). *Transition report: Ten years of transition.* European Bank for Reconstruction and Development.

EBRD. (2009). *Transition report: Transition in crisis ?* European Bank for Reconstruction and Development.

EBRD. (2010). *Transition report: Recovery and reform.* European Bank for Reconstruction and Development.

Farkas, B. (2016). *Models of capitalism in the European Union: Post-crisis perspectives.* Palgrave Macmillan.

IMF. (2009a, January). *Republic of Latvia: Request for stand-by arrangement* (IMF Country Report, n°09/3). International Monetary Fund.

IMF. (2009b, June). *Romania: Request for stand-by arrangement* (IMF Country Report, n°09/183). International Monetary Fund.

Kornai, J. (1980). *Economics of shortage (vol. A and B).* North Holland Publishing Company.

Kornai, J. (1996). *Paying the bill for Goulash-communism—Hungarian development and Macro stabilization in a political-economy perspective* (Discussion papers no. 23). Collegium Budapest/Institute for Advanced Study.

Köves, A. (1992). Shock-Therapy versus gradual change: Economic problems and policies in central and eastern Europe (1989–1991). *Acta Œconomica, 44*(1–2), 15–36.

Lipton, D., & Sachs, J. (1990a). Creating a market economy in Eastern Europe : The case of Poland. *Brooking Papers on Economic Activity*, 1.

Lipton, D., & Sachs, J.(1990b). Privatization in Eastern Europe: The case of Poland. *Brooking Papers on Economic Activity*, 2.

Magnin, E. (1999). *Les transformations économiques en Europe de l'Est depuis 1989, coll.* Dunod.

Magnin, E. (2002). Path-dependence and initial conditions in the transition process: The cases of Hungary and Romania. *East-West Journal of Economics and Business, 5*(1), 67–87.

Magnin, E. (2009). Concurrence fiscale et modèle social dans l'Europe élargie: Convergence ou désunion européenne? *Revue D'études Comparatives Est-Ouest, 40*(2), 55–86.

Mertlik, P. (1997). Czech privatization: From public ownership to public ownership in five years? *Eastern European Economics, 35*(2), 64–83.

Nölke, A., & Vliegenthart A. (2009). Enlarging the variety of capitalism: The emergence of dependent market economies in East Central Europe. *World Politics*, *61*(4), 670–702.

North, D. (1990). *Institutions, institutional change and economic performance.* Cambridge University Press.

Podvrsic, A., & L. Schmidt (2018). From crisis to crisis: Behind the scenes of Peripherisation and Europeanisation of Slovenia. *Revue de la Régulation* [online], 24, 2nd semester/Autumn.

Portes, R. (Ed.). (1993). *Economic transformation in central Europe: A progress report.* CEPR.

Stark, D. (1992). Path dependence and privatization strategies in East Central Europe. *East European Politics and Societies, 6*(1), 17–54.

Stark, D. (1996, January). Recombinant property in East European Capitalism. *American Journal of Sociology, 101*(4).

Stiglitz, J. (1999, April 28–30). Whither reform? Ten years of transition. *Keynote address to the annual bank conference on development economics*, The World Bank.

UNECE. (1992). *Economic survey of Europe in 1991–1992.* United Nations Economic Commission for Europe.

UNECE. (1997). *Economic survey of Europe in 1996–1997.* United Nations Economic Commission for Europe.

UNECE. (1999). *Economic survey of Europe 1999, n°1.* United Nations Economic Commission for Europe.

Williamson, J. (1990). What Washington means by policy reform. In J. Williamson (Ed.), *Latin American adjustment: How much has happened?* chap. 2, Washington: Institute for International Economics.

World Bank. (1996). *From plan to market: World development report.* Oxford University Press.

World Bank. (2002). *Transition the first ten years: Analysis and lessons for Eastern Europe and the Former Soviet Union.* The World Bank.

World Bank. (2005). *Economic growth in the 1990s: Learning from a decade of reform.* The World Bank.

Wagener, H.-J. (2002). The welfare state in transition economies and accession to the EU. *West European Politics, Special Issue, 25*(2), 152–174.

CHAPTER 6

Dependent Monetary Regimes in Post-Communist Balkan Periphery: Currency Boards in Bulgaria and Bosnia and Herzegovina

Abstract In this chapter, we present in a comparative perspective the post-communist economic development of the CEE countries and the Balkans, as well as the central place of the monetary regime in the overall institutional dynamics. Currency boards and official euroization in the countries of the Balkan region have been reconstructed from the standpoint of the model of dependent capitalism and dependent monetary regime. They are a kind of extreme, archetypal form of monetary dependence. The introduction and functioning of Currency boards in Bulgaria and Bosnia and Herzegovina, as well as the euro (DM) as legal tender in Montenegro and Kosovo, are studied. Currency boards and euroization clearly show the role of economic interests and power asymmetries both between actors within countries and between national and international interest groups, the manifestation of geopolitical and geoeconomical dependencies and ambitions. In this chapter, we focus on Currency boards in Bulgaria and Bosnia and Herzegovina, and in the next on euroization of Montenegro and Kosovo.

Keywords Currency Board · Bosnia and Herzegovina · Bulgaria · Economic crisis 1996/1997 · Central bank of Bosnia and Herzegovina · Bulgarian National Bank · Monetary Dependence

E. Magnin and N. Nenovsky, *Diversity of Capitalism in Central and Eastern Europe*, https://doi.org/10.1007/978-3-031-04950-7_6

Introduction: The Second Birth of Capitalism and Monetary Regimes in the Balkans

With the collapse of the communist system, the Balkan countries took on a specific trajectory of development, different from that of Central European (CE) and Baltic countries presented in the previous chapter. In order to understand the dependent monetary regimes in the Balkans in the late 1990s, it is crucial to clarify the initial conditions of the 'transition' (although the term 'transformation' would be more accurate). These conditions are mainly related to (i) the historical and geopolitical factors (the Balkans as a place of confrontation of the great powers, as well as constant interethnic and interstate conflicts), (ii) cultural traditions (the leading role of the state and communitarianism, the lack of long-standing capitalist traditions, etc.) and (iii) the specifics of communism in Balkan countries (which took extremely authoritarian forms in Albania, Romania, partly in Bulgaria, as well as liberal, self-governing and federal manifestations in SFR Yugoslavia) and perceived legacies. As highlighted in the previous chapter, history and path dependence matter.

From the very beginning, the transformation in CE and the Baltics can be defined as 'externally, internationally oriented', aiming at a quick and radical separation from the orbit of the USSR/Russia and a reorientation to Europe/Germany. Quite the opposite, the transformation in the Balkan countries can be defined as 'internally, domestically oriented', largely closed within national borders. The Balkans were dominated by local elites and interests, hesitant in their geopolitical choice between the West and Russia. And while in Central Europe and the Baltics, ideas, values and ideology played an important role, in the Balkans, to use Marx's expression, the 'cash' principles, i.e. gross and short-term interests, reigned.

Furthermore, in the CE and Baltic countries, the sources and methods of privatization were linked to foreign capital, and the shift to market happened very quickly through the so-called shock therapy.[1] These countries had clearly chosen the model of Western-dependent development. Conversely, on the Balkans, former communist elites built a nationally

[1] See Chapter 5. There is an extensive literature on the dynamics of reforms; see, for example, Balcerowicz (1997), Magnin (1999), Winiecki (2004), Aslund (2007), Kornai (2000), Mitrović (2009), Roaf et al. (2014) and IMF (2015), and more recently Andreff (2020), Chepurenko and Szanyi (2021) and Astrov et al. (2021).

encapsulated system of economic, financial and political mechanisms to turn their power resources into financial and economic capital.[2] Privatization and the initial accumulation of capital in these countries were entirely organized in favour of domestic business groups and interests. Overall, the reforms were slow and inconsistent, serving the primitive accumulation of capital.[3] All this allowed a large-scale redistribution of income and resources in favour of the former *nomenklatura*. They gave birth to the new "old" capitalist owners, to whom the words of J. Kornai apply most fully:

> Birds are sitting in a tree. A gun goes off. They all fly into the air and then land again. Each bird may be on a different branch, but the whole flock is back sitting in the tree again. (Kornai, 2000)

The evolution of monetary regimes can be interpreted within the context of the indicated general institutional dynamics. The CE and the Baltics imposed tight monetary regimes and generally fixed exchange rates from the outset in order to attract foreign capital and redirect the monetary regime to the West, especially to Germany.[4] Legally, Currency boards (later in the text CBA for Currency Boards Arrangement) were introduced in Estonia (1992)[5] and Lithuania (1994), and de facto in Latvia (1994). Poland, Czechoslovakia and Hungary also opted for 'early fixing' and their currencies were virtually under regimes similar to CBA for several years. Their currencies were pegged at different times and under different forms to the dollar, to SDR, to the Deutschemark, to currency baskets, etc. 'Exchange stabilization funds' were set up and a conservative monetary policy was pursued.[6] In contrast, in the Balkan countries, monetary regimes were entirely subordinated to fiscal policy, and through

[2] Nenovsky and Mihailova-Borissova (2015).

[3] See Chapter 5.

[4] The radical change of the monetary regime in the Baltic countries has a political and geopolitical character (Abdelal, 2005; Blanc, 2007; Cohen, 1998; Feldmann, 2013).

[5] Estonia is the only country to choose a CBA independently, without external pressure and even against the initial IMF resistance. For modern Currency boards, see Balino and Enoch (1997), Camillieri Gilson (2002), Desquilbet and Nenovsky (2004), Wolf et al. (2008), Cross et al. (2012), for a general picture on exchange rate regimes in Eastern Europe, see Grittersovà (2014), and for the Bulgarian Currency board, Hanke (2012).

[6] The dynamics of monetary regimes is described in Nenovsky et al. (2001) and Nenovsky (2009).

it—to political and private interests. The floating exchange rate and the arbitrary discretionary monetary policy of the Central Bank (various types of bank refinancing and budget financing) were the main levers in these processes. We call these countries 'earlier floaters'.[7]

After the initial accumulation of capital and the formation of the backbone of the private property rights system around 1996/1997, almost all post-communist countries (to varying degrees) experienced financial and political crises that led to a shift in their macroeconomic and monetary frameworks.[8] And while the CE countries began using government intervention more actively and softened their monetary regimes (greater exchange rate flexibility, more active and diverse monetary operations), which generally showed a desire for greater national independence, the Balkan periphery, where the crisis was particularly deep, went in the opposite direction.[9] Under the dictate of economic, financial (especially foreign debt) circumstances, as well as geopolitical and military conflicts (such as the final disintegration of Yugoslavia), the Balkan periphery had to radically and belatedly reorient itself to extreme forms of dependent capitalism, with all its resultant traits (presented in earlier chapters). Monetary regimes were installed, radically limiting national sovereignty, leading to conservative public finances, infiltration of Western capital and banks, a flexible labour market, weak trade unions and so on.

Events unfolded in such a way that dependent monetary regimes (DMR) proved to be a good choice (because they created discipline and trust) in the EU accession process that began almost immediately (a kind of externally set institutional anchor[10]). In fact, the effectiveness and success of the DMR can be judged by the extent to which foreign investment and stability, which the DMR guarantees, are likely

[7] It should be added that monetary substitution has been extremely strong in the Balkans, from the very beginning of the transition until today (OeN, 2015; Windischbauer, 2016).

[8] See Chapter 5.

[9] For details, see Nenovsky (2009), Nenovsky and Mihailova-Borissova (2015), and in general for the post-communist countries see Coats and Skreb (2001) and Barizits (2007).

[10] The relationship between the internal, monetary anchor and the external EU anchor has complex dynamics. In certain periods, they function synchronously (before accession, when there is a common national goal leading to cooperative behaviour). In other periods, they contradict each other (after accession, when the goal is achieved and uncooperative strategies emerge). For details, see Nenovsky and Villieu (2011) and Nenovsky and Ialnazov (2011).

to lead to the relocation of national production to high-tech and leading technology positions in the global and regional value chains. Since then, in one form or another, the Balkan countries have been passively or closely following the ECB's monetary policy. However, following this large political, economic and monetary area, small countries are becoming increasingly dependent on its condition and policies, its problems and its future. And in the last ten years, the state of the EU and the euro area has been a matter of concern.

We now turn to the two extreme cases of DMRs: 'Currency board' and 'unilateral euroization'. How is this choice motivated, as well as the choice of the four countries we will examine: Bulgaria, Bosnia and Herzegovina, Kosovo and Montenegro? Because it could be argued that the selected countries are not representative, but rather extreme cases of state failure and presence of military and ethnic conflicts.

First, in our opinion, the 'extreme' features of these cases make them analytically appropriate: they show in pure, archetypal form the dynamics of domination and the main elements of dependent monetary regimes. Second, all other Balkan countries are only a soft version of these extreme monetary scenarios. We will point out one interesting historical testimony. At the time of the introduction of the mark/euro in Montenegro, according to evidence from that time, Western countries and especially the United States considered this model to be strategically relevant for all Balkan region:

> Montenegro is hailed as an example for the Balkans by Western officials. When, in February of this year, the Montenegrin prime minister visited Washington, U.S. Secretary of State Madeleine Albright 'reinforced U.S. support for the government of Montenegro's efforts on democratisation and economic reform.' At the time the State Department emphasised that Montenegro is 'serving as a model and stimulus for change' in the region. Robert Gelbard, former U.S. envoy to the Balkans, expressed a similar sentiment when he called Montenegro a "guiding light" in his testimony to the Senate Foreign Relations Committee (Dajkovic, 2001, https://zcomm.org/zmagazine/a-model-for-the-balkans-by-alex-n-dajkovic/. The same information was quoted by today's Deputy Governor of the Central Bank of Montenegro, Nikola Fabris, Fabris, 2015, 15)

In fact, the financial crisis in Bulgaria in 1996/1997, which led to the introduction of the Currency board, and the financial and political turmoil in former Yugoslavia that brought about the introduction of the

Currency board in Bosnia and Herzegovina (1994/1998) and euroization of Montenegro (1999) and Kosovo (1999)[11] are evidence of an emergent form of dependent capitalism. Both regimes aim to overcome the so-called inflationary and financial trauma and open up the economy in order to attract foreign capital and financial institutions. They are an extreme form of delegating monetary sovereignty, an entirely outward-oriented monetary regime. In this sixth chapter, we will present Currency boards, and in the next, euroization.

The Currency Board in Bulgaria

Bulgaria is a classic example of introducing and operating a CBA from 1 July 1997. Let us look at the background.

After 1989, Bulgaria's economy took an extremely inefficient trajectory, where ugly forms of crony capitalism emerged. This was expressed in a large-scale appropriation of the state by the former communist *nomenklatura*. Assets and profits of state-owned companies were privatized (i.e. looted) and banks were decapitalized. State-owned enterprises' losses, in turn, were socialized through the budget and automatically monetized by the Central Bank. Monetization took place directly towards the budget or through the banking system. This period was the 'kingdom' of systemic soft budget constraints, which were in fact genetically predetermined by the planned economy.

The monetary regime was built entirely on the expansion of domestic sources of money supply. The various forms of refinancing in lev and foreign currency included discount refinancing using private securities as collateral, Lombard refinancing using government securities as collateral and uncollateralized refinancing (deposit facilities and later arrears). (See detailed statistics on refinancing in Berlemann and Nenovsky, 2004, table on page 225). At the end of June 1996, uncollateralized refinancing was 80% of total lev refinancing and 80% of total foreign currency refinancing

[11] Of course, similar regimes were introduced in the other former Yugoslav republics, including Yugoslavia itself (for a general picture on Yugoslavia, see Lahiri, 1991 and Avramovic, 1995). For example, in Croatia, which practically imitated a Currency board, and the reforms of D. Avramović in Yugoslavia (March 1993–May 1995). These examples are not discussed in the book. For the different interpretations of the break-up of Yugoslavia, see Jovic (2001) and Chossudovsky (1997). For more general information on the dynamics of Balkan countries, see Patrovic (2008) and Mitrović (2009).

and direct budget financing reached colossal amounts (e.g. at the end of 1996 a loan of 7% of GDP was granted to the Ministry of Finance).[12]

The exchange rate was 'actively managed' (against the dollar), however with constant jumps in depreciation, which were in favour of the newly formed speculators and owners. According to Professor Hristina Vutcheva[13] former Minister of Finance, in 1994:

> Every weekend there was an attack on the money market; an agreement was reached among several banks, and the exchange rate was changed in the direction of lev devaluation to ensure safe profits for the players. Then the BNB intervened, buying expensive dollars and so on and so forth till the next hit. (Vutcheva, 2001, 27)

All this 'bad' dynamics led to the depletion of foreign exchange reserves, to a huge accumulation of government debt (reaching 303% of GDP at the end of 1996[14]). Eventually, payments on the external debt stopped and Bulgaria experienced a large-scale banking crisis (Ignatiev, 2005). In May 1996, the base interest rate was 108% (simple annual), in September 1996 it rose to 300%, then it was reduced twice in October 1996 to 240%, and later 180%.[15] The banking crisis automatically led to the devaluation of the lev by 660% in 1996 and 250% only in February 1997 and to soaring inflation (reaching 44% in January and 243% in February 1997).

Altogether, 14 commercial banks (out of 46) were closed in 1996. This represented 24% of the banking system's assets. 90% of uncollateralized refinancing before the 1996/1997 crisis was concentrated in the

[12] The Bulgarian transition and the financial crisis of 1996/1997, briefly summarized in Chapter 5, have been the subject of numerous and detailed analyses and publications in Bulgarian and Western literature (R. Dobrinsky, I. Mihov, G. Minasyan, R. Avramov, K. Stanchev, H. Vutcheva, G. Stanoeva, Z. Balyozov, V. Yotsov, M. Nenova, Ts. Manchev, K. Hristov, N. Valev, P. Ignatiev, S. Petranov, K. Koford, J. Miller, C. Poirot, J. Sgard, M. Berlemann, L. Roussenova, OECD, the Institute for Market Economy in Sofia and many others).

[13] Hristina Vutcheva (1937–2020), a well-known professor of finance and the only woman finance minister in the history of Bulgaria. Author of the book *Economic Policy in Bulgaria during 1991–2000* (2001).

[14] A 60% domestic and 243% external debt.

[15] A critical analysis of a high interest rates policy and of the IMF's stabilisation approach in general is made in Poirot (2003).

bankrupt banks.[16] During 1996, the population withdrew 42% of its foreign currency deposits and 21% of its lev deposits. This was almost 70% of Bulgaria's foreign currency reserves. Depositors lost more than 50% of their savings. The financial crisis was accompanied by a deep political crisis and mass demonstrations, not without the intervention of external forces and IFIs (Roussenova, 2002). The social turmoil culminated on 10 January 1997 when the Parliament was attacked. After the election, a new, right-wing political force came to power. It was backed by strong external players—the major Western governments, the IMF and foreign banks, Bulgaria's main creditors. The IMF role was crucial: it constructed the new monetary regime as part of the stabilization program for Bulgaria[17] The importance of the IMF and of the political support for the Currency board is evident from a statement of the senior official of the Economic Commission, Michael Deppler, to the Bulgarian Parliament before the CBA introduction:

> You lost seven years! [...] We want from Bulgarian politicians total commitment and determination that the model would function for an indefinitely long time in the future, as long as it is necessary. (Deppler, 1996, 9–10)

Although external players were initiators of the monetary regime change, it also crystallized as a result of convergence of interests of almost all other actors (the government, the BNB, the banks surviving the crisis, the newly emerged businesses, etc.). Most importantly, the new regime was supported by households, which suffered the bulk of the losses during the crisis, and which had an interest in the new money-stabilizing

[16] Cumulative expenditures for overcoming the banking crisis of 1991–1998 reached 38.3% of GDP.

[17] Of course, the role of a number of individual actions should also be noted, such as that of Prof. S. Hanke, an active CBA proponent and specialist, who became an adviser to President P. Stoyanov. In fact, S. Hanke, as part of the Run-Up team, proposed a CBA arrangement for Bulgaria as early as 1991 (together with K. Schuler, he published a special text, Hanke & Schuler, 1991). Another of his books, also written in co-authorship with K. Schuler, was translated in 1997 into Bulgarian. For more information, see the memoirs of Steve Hanke (2016). Hanke played a crucial role in imposing the idea of a CBA and euroization on the Balkans, not only in Bulgaria but also in Bosnia and Herzegovina and Montenegro. His memories are documented in Hanke (2016). The importance of leading economists in changing the monetary regime is indisputable, such as is the role of Stanley Fisher, IMF First Deputy Managing Director (1994–2001).

Table 6.1 BNB balance sheets

Assets	*Liabilities*
Issue department balance sheet	
Cash and accounts in foreign currency	Currency in circulation
Monetary gold	Bank deposits and current accounts
Foreign securities	Government deposits and accounts
	Banking Department deposit
Banking department balance sheet	
Non-monetary gold and other precious metals	Borrowings from IMF
Investment in securities	Liabilities to other international financial organizations
Loans and advances to banks	Capital
Claims on government	Reserves
Bulgarian's IMF quota and holdings in other international financial organizations	Retained profit
Deposit within the Issue Department	

Source BNB

regime.[18] In macroeconomic terms, it was clear and research proved that the leading variable, which fuelled inflation expectations and which had to be "anchored", was the exchange rate.[19]

The official introduction of the CBA took place on 1 July 1997, but its prior announcement sharply reduced inflation as early as March when it became clear that a CBA arrangement was on the agenda. The new monetary institution started with a new balance sheet in which the government's domestic debt was zero (inflation had 'done the main work'). Similar to the Estonian Central Bank and historically to the Bank of England, the BNB balance sheet was divided into two parts: Issue Department (Currency Board) and Banking Department (residual LOLR, represented by the deposit in the Banking Department's assets, see Table 6.1). In addition, the Bulgarian National Bank (BNB) regulatory and supervisory functions were preserved, which proved to be extremely

[18] A theoretical and empirical analysis of the dynamics of change of the monetary regime from the positions of the key players, grouped as debtors and creditors, was made in two articles of Nenovsky and Rizopoulos (2003, 2004).

[19] See the empirical study in Nenovsky (1999).

useful in limiting credit growth and with respect to the tendencies for capital movements within foreign banking groups.

With the new law on the BNB, the exchange rate was fixed to the Deutsche Mark (1 DM = 1000 BGL), and the monetary base was covered 100% with highly liquid foreign assets. Any discretionary policy and any kind of refinancing of the government and banks (except in a systemic crisis, and within the residual, above the monetary base, foreign exchange reserve) were prohibited. Thus, the creation of money became disconnected from politics, and hard budgetary and monetary constraints were introduced. Later, the lev was redenominated (1000 BGL became 1 New Bulgarian leva/BGN) and automatically re-pegged to the euro. Thus, today, 23 years later, the level of the exchange rate remains unchanged (1 EURO = 1.95583 BGN) and the monetary base is always 100%, and even more, covered. Today, the CBA is perhaps the only institution for which there is a political consensus despite episodes of strong political instability and social tension. The Bulgarian lev draws credibility from the euro, which is at the top layers of the international currency pyramid[20] The lev has become part of the zone, of the euro geography, and the Bulgarian currency has gained in terms of liquidity.

In macroeconomic terms, almost all elements of the model of dependent and externally oriented capitalism are present: (i) conservative public finances with low debt and years of budget surpluses[21]; (ii) low taxes (and a flat 10% income tax) and low social security charges; (iii) flexible labour market and low trade union presence; (iv) inflow of foreign capital and banks; and (v) relocation of leading European companies in the low-skilled labour segment (see Table 6.2 and Chapter 4; see also Table 3.2, Chapter 3). This is accompanied by monetarist and liberal ideas and relevant translated literature.

Over time, and especially after 2008, it became clear that foreign banks could be a "double-edged sword". In addition to stability and the inflow of needed investments, they can cause credit bubbles (IMF, 2015) or quickly end their commitments (Chapter 5). Despite the specifics of the interaction of EU accession (the ambivalent impact of EU funds), as well as the criticism of slow income growth, etc., in general, it can be claimed

[20] However, a loss of credibility of the euro immediately leads to a loss of credibility of the lev.

[21] The link between a Currency board and a strict fiscal discipline is confirmed by empirical studies (e.g. Grigonyté, 2003).

Table 6.2 Bulgaria and Bosnia and Herzegovina: Main macroeconomic indicators (2000–2019)

	2000	*2005*	*2010*	*2015*	*2019*
Economic growth, %, y/y change					
Bosnia and Herzegovina	5,50	8,76	0,87	3,09	2,68
Bulgaria	4,78	7,15	0,56	3,99	3,69
Inflation, consumer prices (annual %)					
Bosnia and Herzegovina	na	na	2,00	−1,04	0,56
Bulgaria	10,32	5,04	2,44	−0,10	3,10
Net lending (+)/net borrowing (−) (% of GDP)					
Bosnia and Herzegovina	na	1,71	−1,99	0,77	1,71
Bulgaria	−1,53	1,38	−2,04	−0,74	1,92
Debt/GDP, %					
Bosnia and Herzegovina	34,70	25,50	40,80	45,50	33,30
Bulgaria	73,90	28,70	14,10	25,60	19,20
Total reserves (% of total external debt)					
Bosnia and Herzegovina	17,79	36,35	30,87	34,66	43,42
Bulgaria	29,21	46,99	33,97	54,86	68,89
Total reserves in months of imports					
Bosnia and Herzegovina	1,41	3,77	5,81	6,29	7,32
Bulgaria	5,06	4,74	7,10	7,54	7,56
Profit tax (% of commercial profits)					
Bosnia and Herzegovina	na	22,10	5,60	7,20	8,40
Bulgaria	na	7,00	4,70	5,00	4,90
Corporate tax rate, %					
Bosnia and Herzegovina	na	na	10,00	10,00	10,00
Bulgaria	32,50	15,00	10,00	10,00	10,00
Deposit interest rate (%)					
Bosnia and Herzegovina	na	3,56	3,16	2,06	0,91
Bulgaria	3,14	3,08	4,08	0,61	0,02
Lending interest rate (%)					
Bosnia and Herzegovina	na	9,61	7,89	5,79	3,29
Bulgaria	11,34	8,66	11,14	7,45	4,55
Foreign direct investment, net inflows (% of GDP)					
Bosnia and Herzegovina	2,65	5,56	2,58	2,36	1,94
Bulgaria	7,56	13,72	3,66	4,30	2,19

(continued)

Table 6.2 (continued)

	2000	*2005*	*2010*	*2015*	*2019*
Foreign reserves /GDP (constant 2010 US$)					
Bosnia and Herzegovina	4,39	17,07	25,42	25,55	33,94
Bulgaria	25,99	30,90	33,94	44,79	40,60
Net Domestic Credit, %, y/y					
Bosnia and Herzegovina	5,43	28,28	5,90	2,87	5,54
Bulgaria	31,04	32,68	5,14	2,24	11,44
House prices, %, y/y					
Bosnia and Herzegovina	na	na	−1,88	2,09	2,96
Bulgaria	na	na	−10,17	2,79	6,02
Expenditure on education/total expenditures					
Bosnia and Herzegovina	na	na	na	na	na
Bulgaria	10,06	10,88	9,89	9,76	9,98
Foreign bank assets/total assets					
Bosnia and Herzegovina	na	87,0	89,0	na	na
Bulgaria	na	76,0	80,7	76,4	78,3
Minimum wages, USD					
Bosnia and Herzegovina	na	na	na	na	na
Bulgaria	37,60	104,50	176,80	213,10	327,90

Sources World Bank, IMF, Eurostat, Bulgarian NSI, Global Economy, Country Economy

that Currency board is a successful monetary regime (a general picture of the economic development of Bulgaria and Bosnia and Herzegovina is shown in Table 6.2).

The Currency Board in Bosnia and Herzegovina

The second institutional case we will examine is the CBA introduction in *Bosnia and Herzegovina* (1994/1998). Unlike Bulgaria, in addition to financial and monetary problems, military and geopolitical factors also played a major role here. Bosnia and Herzegovina emerges as 'a unique experience on the practical organisation of a modern protectorate system, the lessons of which need to be drawn' (CEPS, 1999, 24).[22] The CBA was a stabilizing institution imposed from outside in order to protect the

[22] See Chandler (1999) for details. The CBA in Bosnia and Herzegovina is the subject of a number of publications. In addition to those listed below, we would like to note the collection edited by D. Kovacevic (2004) (especially the articles of W. Coats, P. Nicholl, J. Hawkins, W. Salater, A. Winkler and A. Mehl, Ž. Šević and D. Ćosić), as well as the

strategic interests of the leading geopolitical actors, as well as to anchor the political infighting.

As known, in December 1995, the Dayton Peace Agreement was signed near Dayton in Ohio (Gilbert & Mujanović, 2015). It put an end to the open conflict with many victims (about 250,000 killed, 3–4 million displaced and $100 billion in total losses), which after the break-up of Yugoslavia opposed the three ethnic communities—Serbs (Orthodox Christians), Bosnians (Muslims) and Croats (Catholics).

The CBA had to economically and technically unite the three monetary areas and the three monetary authorities[23] that existed until then. In fact, between 1992 and 1995, there was monetary chaos.[24] After the independence of Bosnia and Herzegovina was announced in March 1992, the payment community started to disintegrate and several currencies were put into circulation, depending on the actors' ethnic and trade preferences (various types of emergency currencies alongside with officially accepted *Novcani Bons*, Deutsche Mark, Serbian Dinar, Croatian Dinar and *Kuna*). The situation became also complicated by the hyperinflation in Yugoslavia, as well as the fact that the payment system ('payment transactions bureau' of the three zones) was located in Belgrade (Coats, 2007b).[25] In August 1994, the Currency board was introduced in the Bosnian territory after the Bosnian Dinar was redenominated and subsequently pegged to the Deutsche Mark at an exchange rate of 100 new dinars = 1 DM. The new currency was backed 100% with marks. In

collection for the CBA's 20th anniversary, in K. Kosarića ed., (notably the articles of P. Nicholl, D. Demekas and M. Chivakul). See also Gedeon (2013).

[23] The National Bank of Bosnia and Herzegovina, the National Bank of Republika Srpska and the Mostar ZAP (in the Croatian-majority region) (Kamhi & Deheija, 2006, 48).

[24] The most comprehensive monetary history of the region was written by Warren Coats (2007a, 2007b) who was a representative of the IMF mission in Bosnia and Herzegovina during the construction of the new monetary system. In his publications, Coats presents extremely interesting testimonies and documents showing the role and strategy of the leading actors. These books also contain extremely interesting technical information about the monetary systems. Discussions on the shape of banknotes and the symbols on them are also presented; as we pointed out in Chapter 3, banknotes are an important symbolic and communication channel for the exercise of sovereignty.

[25] The three payment bureaux (ZPP, SPP and ZAP) were part of the Yugoslav Payment and Accounting System SDK (Yugoslav Service for Social Bookkeeping). Coats describes in detail the importance of the payment and clearing system for building an independent monetary regime. See also Tesche (2000).

general, on the eve of Dayton, there were three monetary zones, all of which closely linked to the Deutsche Mark (CBA in Bosnia, fixed exchange rates of the kuna in the Croatian zone and the Serbian Dinar in the Serbian zone).

An annex to the Dayton Agreement (No. 4) and the new constitution of Bosnia and Herzegovina (Article 7) specifically address the monetary system and the Central Bank of the new political community. Kovacevic clearly formulated the situation in 1997:

> When the Central Bank of Bosnia and Herzegovina (CBBH) started its operations in August 1997, the country faced, and largely still faces today, three major concurrent transition processes: (i) the transition from war to peace; (ii) the transition from a socialist command economy dominated by the state to a market oriented private sector economy; and (iii) the transition from being a part of a larger nation to being an independent country with its own democratic and administrative institutions. Any one of these transition processes on its own is extremely challenging. Within this avalanche of change there is a need to provide some anchors or areas of economic stability at an early stage of the reform process. One such anchor, which the experience of Bosnia and Herzegovina shows can be attained successfully and relatively quickly, is a stable currency. (Kovacevic, 2003, 59)

For its part, Article 7 clearly illustrates the nature of the dependent monetary regime:

> "There shall be a Central Bank of Bosnia and Herzegovina, which shall be the sole authority for issuing currency and for monetary policy throughout Bosnia and Herzegovina.
>
> 1. The Central Bank's responsibilities will be determined by the Parliamentary Assembly. For the first six years after the entry into force of this Constitution, however, it may not extend credit by creating money, operating in this respect as a Currency board; thereafter, the Parliamentary Assembly may give it that authority.
> 2. The first Governing Board of the Central Bank shall consist of a Governor appointed by the International Monetary Fund, after consultation with the Presidency, and three members appointed by the Presidency, two from the Federation (one Bosniac, one Croat, who shall share one vote) and one from the Republika Srpska, all of whom shall serve a six-year term. The Governor, who shall not be

a citizen of Bosnia and Herzegovina or any neighbouring state, may cast tie-breaking votes on the Governing Board.

3. Thereafter, the Governing Board of the Central Bank of Bosnia and Herzegovina shall consist of five persons appointed by the Presidency for a term of six years. The Board shall appoint, from among its members, a Governor for a term of six years." (http://www.ccbh.ba/osnovni-akti/ustav/?title=clan-7&lang=en)

The CBA construction was assigned entirely to the IMF with representatives of the leading CBs also participating in the technical missions (accounting, payment system, etc.) (Coats, 2007a). The law on the new bank was adopted by Parliament on 20 June 1997, and the bank began operations on 11 August of that year. Under the pressure of the IMF, the US Treasury and a number of Western European countries, a decision was made to establish a common Currency board, integrating the three zones[26] and a new currency, called Convertible Mark/*Konvertibilna Marka* (KM), was put into circulation (from June 1998 1DM = 1 km, and since 2002 1 EUR = 1.95583 km). Also, a stand-alone, independent of Serbia, clearing system was set up (launched in early 2001).

The CBA in Bosnia and Herzegovina, as a construction and as a practice, is an extremely and orthodox dependent monetary regime[27] Within the first 6 years, the Governor was appointed by the IMF: he could not be a local resident or a resident of the neighbouring countries (the first Governor was the Frenchman Serge Robert, and the second—the New Zealander Peter Nicholl).[28] The three deputy governors were representatives of the two political communities, two from the Federation of Bosnia and Herzegovina and one from the Serb Republic (Republika Srpska), with the first two sharing one vote. In 2003, a political decision was adopted to keep the Currency board and make it a permanent monetary regime.

[26] The other options were introducing the DM as an official currency or creating three mutually interrelated CBAs (Coats, 2007a). See also Softić, S. (2017).

[27] In the first year, there was no full coverage of the monetary base and the bank started with zero capital (waiting for a tranche from the IMF), but this was quickly overcome (Nicholl, 2008). See the interesting political frictions on this subject (the letter of the Serbian representatives in the CBA to the IMF Managing Director M. Camdessus) presented in Coats (2007a).

[28] Subsequently, after the first term of office, the governors were local residents: first—Kemal Kozarić—and presently—Senad Softić.

The bank has no relationship with the government (apart from being its fiscal agent), and its only instruments for influencing banks are required reserves and free reserves. The latter are regulated by certain requirements for matching of maturities by assets and liabilities, and the interest rates paid on them. Unlike in Bulgaria, the law does not envisage the existence of even a residual LOLR, and banking supervision is outside the Currency board (in a separate agency). According to an interview conducted by the researcher E. Abuannab:

> A senior official in the CBBH states that although *de jure* the CBBH is only allowed to use required reserves, *de facto* there is another type of instrument present: "Although required reserve is essentially a credit expansion control instrument, it's also in a way a reserve of liquidity for crisis situations. As the CBBH is not a lender of last resort for commercial banks, this represents a breach of required reserve control. Therefore, the CBBH relies on this instrument, namely bank liquidity regulation. This was demonstrated quite clearly during the 2008 crisis. (Interview 4) (Abuannab, 2019, 41)

The banking system is dominated by almost 90% of foreign banks (Austrian, German and Italian).[29] From 1997 to 2014, the seigniorage grew, and from 2004, in addition to the capital increase (in 1997 the bank started without capital), a contribution was made to the budget. Strong current account deficits are offset by capital inflows (including from privatization) and especially from large remittances of emigrants. It is interesting to note that the four countries with dependent regimes that are presented in this chapter are at the forefront of revenue from remittances in Europe and hence belong to the variety of dependent capitalism which depends on remittances (see Chapter 5).

Confidence in the new currency was strong; it quickly overcame the "inflation trauma". According to the empirical study of Begovic et al. (2016), confidence in the national currency in Bosnia and Herzegovina

[29] As early as 2008, it was noted that the Austrian banks held 60% of the banking system's assets and this represents a certain vulnerability (Demekas & Chivakul, 2008, 41–44).

(as well as in Bulgaria) is due to the credibility of the Currency board, and the greater it is, the lower the confidence in the government.[30]

> The results of the empirical analysis suggest that the effect of CBA on expectations about the local currency stability and trustworthiness is positive and significant. Moreover, we find that the positive effect of CBA is greater the worse the expectations about economic prospects and the lower the trust in government. The survey evidence reported earlier suggests that respondents from countries with currency boards are systematically less optimistic/more pessimistic about their country's medium-term economic prospects and about as trusting/distrusting in government as are respondents from transition economies with other monetary regimes. (Begovic et al., 2016, 799)

As for discipline and 'automatism', according to Steve Hanke, the Currency board in Bosnia and Herzegovina is the closest to the orthodox form—the value of its sterilization rate, which shows the monetary authorities' capacity to influence the monetary base, approximates zero.[31] The official exit from the Currency board is seen in joining the euro area and no mention is made of an independent monetary policy.

In addition, the Currency board in Bosnia and Herzegovina is an eloquent evidence that dependence on foreign banks and their capital can grow into a threat. These capitals, in the absence of adequate risk mitigation mechanisms, can lead to a strong increase in credit[32] and seriously challenge the LOLR function in a crisis, as well as the very existence of the Currency board. The crisis in 2008 is best described by Sh. Gedeon:

> Once a long-term corporate or real estate loan has been negotiated, the Bosnian subsidiary moves foreign assets (secondary reserves) to the parent bank abroad to serve as collateral against a loan that the parent bank will now create for the subsidiary. This loan appears as new foreign liabilities of

[30] Another survey shows that despite stable expectations for 'no devaluation' of the lev, this does not lead to full credibility of the Currency board in Bulgaria (Valev & Carlson, 2007).

[31] Hanke (2002b). According to evidence, Hanke was initially critical of the IMF project because it left room for discretion (see Coats, 2007a; Hanke, 2016). Empirical evidence of the Currency board orthodoxy is also the high correlations of monetary authority foreign assets with the currency in circulation, the monetary base and the broad money, calculated by Hawkins (2004, 53).

[32] IMF (2015). See also Chapter 5.

> the commercial bank. The bank can sell some of the foreign exchange to the currency board, holding the domestic currency as reserves against the new foreign liabilities while the currency board shows an equal increase of its foreign currency assets against the new increase in reserves. In this process the consolidated balance sheet for the commercial banks shows an increase in foreign liabilities, and the balance sheet of the currency board show an increase in assets. This is the process that Goodfriend and King (1988) term "unsterilized discount window lending." It explains how the broad money supply grew by over 20% each year since 2000. (Gedeon, 2010, 13)

> The fourth quarter of 2008 was most dramatic. During the fourth quarter of 2008, foreign exchange reserves of the currency board contracted by 8% - the largest decline recorded in a single quarter. This was due to the 17% drop in bank reserves (KM 705 million) from the withdrawal of deposits from the banks. The decrease of foreign exchange brought about a fourth quarter contraction of the monetary base by 9% and a contraction of the broad money supply, M2, by 4.8%. Compared to the second quarter of 2008 which saw a 5 percent increase in the broad money supply, the "whiplash" was significant: a quarterly decline in M2 of 9.8 percent. (Gedeon, 2010, 15)

It was in this critical situation, under the influence of IFIs and private banks, that the Vienna Initiative was launched, in which Western private banks undertook to capitalize their subsidiaries in Bosnia and Herzegovina. This was accompanied by a stabilization loan of 1.6 billion USD from the IMF (in order to preserve the CBA). The 2008 crisis clearly shows that various forms of LOLR (ex post or ex ante) need to be considered, as well as bank regulations to limit lending, risk exposures and capital outflows to parent banks.[33]

Concluding Comments

The CBA is a typical representative of the DMR. Normally, it is introduced after a deep monetary and political crisis, and the monetary dynamics in the country is completely subordinated to an external monetary centre, to a leading central bank. The CBA places strict limits on

[33] Bulgaria is a good example of such regulatory intervention (both before 2008 when there was a credit boom and in 2009 when the capital requirements of foreign banks changed).

moral hazard in the monetary and fiscal spheres, refusing to finance government and banks (Vukčević & Jovović, 2019). The legally fixed exchange rate, the coverage of the monetary base and free convertibility become the main anchors of trust and credibility. This attracts foreign capital and generally increases the competitiveness and technological level of the national economy. Of course, the positive effects of the introduction of a CBA can be developed by supporting a common institutional and political environment. This is illustrated by the experience of Bulgaria and Bosnia and Herzegovina.

And while the CBA, as a dependent monetary regime, retains some attributes of monetary sovereignty, euroization goes a step further. We will quote E. Abuannab again regarding the Bosnia and Herzegovina choice of CBA over euroization:

> In a matter of about a year, Governor Nicholl expressed satisfaction with the level of confidence of the population into the domestic currency. "Bosnia could have chosen to adopt the DM... But instead, they picked to have a domestic currency tied 1:1 to the DM. The main reason was that the new country needed symbols of its existence and unity. Having its own currency is one such symbol" (Nicholl, 1999). A senior representative of the CBBH makes a similar claim: "The emission of our own currency is without a doubt an expression of sovereignty, statehood, legal continuity and identity of Bosnia and Herzegovina" (Interview 3). (Abuannab, 2019, 49)

Under the regime of euroization, the monetary dependence is more pronounced—there is even a lack of basic symbols of a nation-state and political sovereignty.[34] In the next chapter, we turn to the presentation of euroization, reconstructing the history of the introduction of the euro (DM) in Montenegro and Kosovo.

References

Aslund, A. (2007). *How the capitalism was built: The transformation of Central and Eastern Europe, Russia, and Central Asia*. Cambridge University Press.

Astrov, V., Grinberg, R., Inozemtsev, V., Kochnev, A. (2021). *Special issue 30th anniversary of the break-up of the USSR* (WIIW Monthly Report No. 12).

[34] Helleiner (2003, Ch. 5). For detailed explanation about monetary sovereignty and its legal aspects, see Zafiroski (2018, 49–72).

Abdelal, R. (2005). *National purpose in the world economy. Post-Soviet states in comparative perspective*. Cornell University Press.

Abuannab, E. (2019). *Structural constraints and choice in monetary policy regime design: Bosnia and Kosovo in comparative perspective*. İhsan Doğramacı Bilkent University.

Andreff, W. (Ed.). (2020). *Comparative economic studies in Europe: A thirty-year review studies in economic transition*. Springer Nature.

Avramovic, D. (1995). *Reconstruction of the Monetary System and Economic Recovery of Yugoslavia, Analytical framework, results and problems* (WIIW Research Reports, N° 216).

Balcerowicz, L. (1997). *Socjalizm. Kapitalizm. Transformacja. Szkice z przełomu epok*. PWN.

Balino, T., & Enoch, C. (Eds.). (1997). *Currency board arrangements: Issues and experiences* (IMF Occasional Paper No. 151). International Monetary Fund.

Barisitz, S. B. S. (2007). Exchange rate arrangements and monetary policy in Southeastern Europe: An update (2004–2007). *OeNB Focus on European Economic Integration, 2*(7), 78–99.

Begović, S., Adnett, N., & Pugh, G. (2016). An investigation into the credibility of currency board arrangements in Bosnia and Herzegovina and Bulgaria. *Journal of Comparative Economics, Elsevier, 44*(3), 787–799.

Berlemann, M., & Nenovsky, N. (2004). Lending of first versus lending of last resort: The Bulgarian financial crisis of 1996/1997. *Comparative Economic Studies, 46*(2), 245–271.

Blanc, J. (2007). La monnaie comme projet politique: restauration monétaire et currency board en Lituanie, 1988–1994. In B. Théret (Ed.), *La monnaie dévoilée par ses crises. Crises monétaires d'hier et d'aujourd'hui* (pp. 401–428). Editions de l'EHESS.

Camillieri Gilson, M.-T. (2002). *Policy pre-commitment and institutional design: A synthetic indicator applied to Currency Boards* (OECD working paper N 16).

Chandler, D. (1999). *Bosnia: Faking democracy after Dayton*. Pluto Press.

Chepurenko, A., & Szanyi, M. (2021). *Parallel processes and divergent outcomes: The transformation of the economies of former Socialist countries* (Leibniz-Institut für Ost- und Südosteuropaforschung Working Papers No. 393)

CEPS. (1999). *A system for Post-War South-East Europe (Plan for Reconstruction, Openness, Development and Integration)* (Centre for European Policy Studies WP N° 131).

Coats, W. (2007a). *One currency for Bosnia*. Ottawa, Jameson Books Inc.

Coats, W. (2007b). Monetary policy issues in post conflict economies, New York University's Center on International Cooperation (J. K. Boyce & M. O'Donnell, Eds.). Rienner. http://works.bepress.com/cgi/viewcontent.cgi?article=1008&context=warren_coats

Coats, W., & Skreb, M. (2001). Central banking in transition: An overview of main ten years after, Revue d'économie financière. In Special issue: *Ten years of transformation in Eastern European countries. Achievements and challenges* (pp. 265–286), AEF.

Cohen, B. (1998). *The geography of money*. Cornel University Press.

Chossudovsky, M. (1997). Dismantling former Yugoslavia: Recolonising Bosnia. *Development in Practice, 7*(4), 375–383.

Cross, T., Heft, J. & Rodgers, D. (2012). *On currency boards—An updated bibliography of scholarly writings*. Johns Hopkins Institute for Applied Economics, Global Health, and Study of Business Enterprise Currency Board Working Paper No. 1.

Dajkovic, A. (2001). *A «Model» for the Balkans*. https://zcomm.org/zmagazine/a-model-for-the-balkans-by-alex-n-dajkovic/

Demekas, D., & Chivakul, M. (2008). Managing financial stability in Bosnia & Herzegovina. In K. Kozarić (Ed.), *Monetary stability in the function of financial stability* (pp. 41–44). Edition CBBH.

Deppler, M. (1996). The Deppler's ultimatum. *The Banker*, (45), 9–10 (in Bulgarian).

Desquilbet, J. B., & Nenovsky, N. (2004). *Credibility and adjustment: Gold standards and currency boards compared* (*William Davidson Institute WP* N° 692).

Fabris, N. (2015). The history of money in Montenegro. *Journal of Central Banking Theory and Practice, 4*(1), 5–18.

Feldmann, M. (2013). From the ruble zone to the Euro Zone: The political economy of Estonian macroeconomic policy. *Post-Soviet Affairs, 29*(4), 354–370.

Gedeon, Sh. (2010). The political economy of currency boards: Case of Bosnia and Herzegovina. *South East European Journal of Economics and Business, 5*(2), 7–20.

Gedeon, Sh. (2013). Stability properties of the currency board: Case study of Bosnia and Herzegovina 2004–2010. *Bank and Bank Systems, 8*(3), 87–99.

Gilbert, A., & Mujanović, J. (2015). Dayton at twenty: Towards new politics in Bosnia-Herzegovina. *Southeast European and Black Sea Studies, 15*(4), 605–610.

Grigonytė, D. (2003). Impact of currency boards on fiscal policy in Central and Eastern European countries. *Economic Change and Restructuring, 36*(2), 111–133.

Grittersovà, J. (2014). Exchange rates in transition economies. In Th. Oatley (Ed.), *The international political economy of the international monetary and financial system*. Edward Elgar.

Hanke, S. (1996/1997). A field report from Sarajevo and Pale. *Central Banking, 7*(3), 36–40.

Hanke, S. (2002a). Currency boards. *Annals of American Academy of Political and Social Science, 579*, 87–105.

Hanke, S. (2002b). On dollarization and currency boards: Error and deception. *Policy Reform, 5*(4), 203–222.

Hanke, S. (2012). *Bulgaria: Fifteen years later. Currency Board* (Global Health, and Study of Business Enterprise Currency Board Working Paper No. 2). Johns Hopkins Institute for Applied Economics.

Hanke, S., & Schuler, K. (1991). *Teeth for the Bulgarian Lev: A currency board solution*. International Freedom Foundation.

Hawkins, J. (2004). Flexibility and currency boards. In D. Kovačević (Ed.), *Modern-Day currency boards. Practice and prospects* (pp. 37–67). CBBH.

Henke, S. (2016). *Remembrances of a currency reformer: Some notes and sketches from the field* (Global Health, and Study of Business Enterprise Currency Board WP No. 55). Johns Hopkins Institute for Applied Economics.

Ignatiev, P. (2005). *Banking crisis in Bulgaria in 1996–1997*. Siela, Sofia (in Bulgarian).

IMF. (2015). *The Western Balkans: 15 years of economic transition*, Regional Economic Issues Special Report, IMF.

Jovic, D. (2001). The disintegration of Yugoslavia: A critical review of explanatory approaches. *European Journal of Social Theory, 4*(1), 101–120.

Kamhi, N., & Deheija, V. (2006). An assessment of the currency board regime in Bosnia and Herzegovina. *Emerging Markets Finance and Trade, 42*(6), 46–58.

Koford, K. & Tschoegl, A. E. (1999). Problems of bank lending in Bulgaria: Information asymmetry and institutional learning. *MOCT-MOST: Economic Policy in Transitional Economies, 9*, 123–151.

Koford, K. (2000). Citizen restraints on '"Leviathan"' government: Transition politics in Bulgaria. *European Journal of Political Economy, 16*, 307–338.

Kornai, J. (2000). What the change of system from socialism to capitalism does and does not mean. *Journal of Economic Perspectives, 14*(1), 27–42.

Kovačević, D. (Ed.). (2004). *Modern-day currency boards*. Practice and Prospects.

Kovačević, D. (2003). The currency board and monetary stability in Bosnia and Herzegovina, *BIS WP* N°, *17*, 59–61.

Kozarić, K. (Ed.). (2008). *Monetary stability in the function of financial stability*. Edition CBBH.

Kozarić, K. (2007). *Modeli monetarne politike sa osvrtom na valutni odbor Bosne i Hercegovine* [Models of monetary policy with reference to the Currency Board of Bosnia and Herzegovina]. Specijalne teme istraživanja, Centralna banka Bosne i Hercegovine.

Lahiri, A. (1991). *Money and inflation in Yugoslavia* (IMF Working Paper N° 91/50).

Magnin, E. (1999). *Les transformations économiques en Europe de l'Est depuis 1989*, coll. Les Topos, Dunod.
Mitrović, L. (2009). *Tranzicija u periferni kapitalizam: (ogledi iz sociologije globalnih regionalnih promena)*. Inst. za Političke Studije.
National Bank of Serbia (NBS). (2015, March). Report on the dinarization of the Serbian financial system. National Bank of Serbia.
Nenovsky, N. (1999). Une économie en transition a-t-elle vraiment besoin d'une Banque centrale? La Caisse d'émission en Bulgarie. *Revue d'études comparatives Est-Ouest, 30*(4), 65–96.
Nenovsky, N. (2009). *Monetary regimes in Post-Communist Countries: Some long-term reflections* (Working Paper No.2). Agency for Economic Analysis and Forecasting.
Nenovsky, N., Hristov, K., & Mihaylov, M. (2001). Comparing currency board automatic mechanism in Bulgaria, Estonia and Lithuania. *Journal des Economistes et des Etudes Humaines, 11*(4), 575–616.
Nenovsky, N., & Ialnazov, D. (2011). A game theory interpretation of the post-communist evolution. *Journal of Economic Issues, 45*(1), 41–55.
Nenovsky, N., & Mihaylova Borisova, G. (2015). Debts, ideas and interests in the Balkans. Chronology of the post-communist Transformation, 1990–2013. *Economie et Institutions, 23*(2), 121–145.
Nenovsky, N., & Rizopoulos, Y. (2003). Extreme monetary regime change. Evidence from the Currency Board Introduction in Bulgaria. *Journal of Economic Issues, 37*(4), 909–941.
Nenovsky, N., Tochkov, K., & Turcu, C. (2013). Monetary regime and EU accession: Comparing Bulgaria and Romania. *Communist and Post-Communist Studies, 46*(1), 13–23.
Nenovsky, N., & Villieu, P. (2011). EU Enlargement and monetary regimes from the insurance model perspectives. *Post-Communist Economies, 23*(4), 433–447.
Nicholl, P. (1999). *Comments by Peter Nicholl, Governor of the Central Bank of Bosnia and Herzegovina*. Retrieved from https://www.cbbh.ba.
Nicholl, P. (2008). The development of the CBBH. In K. Kozarić (Ed.), *Monetary stability in the function of financial stability* (pp. 13–20). Edition CBBH.
OeN. (2015). *The Euro in Central, Eastern and South-eastern Europe*. Euro Survey. Austrian Central Bank.
Petrovic, M. (2008). The role of geography and history in determining the slower progress of Post-communist transition in the Balkans. *Communist and Post-Communist Studies, 41*, 123–145.
Poirot, C. (2003). Did the currency board resolve Bulgaria's financial crisis of 1996–97? *Journal of Post Keynesian Economics, 26*(1), 27–55.

Roaf, J., Ayoyan, R., Joshi, B., & Krogulski, K. (Eds.). (2014). *25 years of transition. Post-Communist Europe and the IMF (Special report)*. International Monetary Fund.

Roussenova, L. (2002, April). *The 1996–1997 financial crisis in Bulgaria*, International Seminar on Comparative Experiences in Confronting Banking Sector Problems in Central/Eastern Europe. http://pdc.ceu.hu/archive/00001649/01/crisis-1996-1997-revised-final.pdf

Softić, S. (Ed.). (2017). *Central Bank of Bosnia and Herzegovina. 20 years of stability, 1997–2017*. Central Bank of Bosnia and Herzegovina.

Tesche, J. (2000). Bosnia and Herzegovina: The Post-Dayton economy and financial system. *MOCT-MOST, 3–4*, 311–324.

Valev, N., & Carlson, J. (2007). Beliefs about exchange-rate stability: Survey evidence from the currency board in Bulgaria. *Journal of Economic Policy Reform, 10*(2), 111–121.

Vukčević, I., & Jovović, R. (2019). The quality of public finance in the countries of South-East Europe. *Journal of Central Banking Theory and Practice, 9*(1), 169–184.

Vutcheva, H. (2001). *Economic policy in Bulgaria during 1991—2000*. Stopanstvo Editions (in Bulgarian).

Winiecki, J. (2004). Determinants of catching up or falling behind: Interaction of formal and informal institutions. *Post-Communist Economies, 16*(2), 137–152.

Windischbauer, U. (2016). *Strengthening the role of local currencies in EU candidate and potential candidate countries* (ECB Occasional Paper N° 170).

Wolf, H., Gnosh, A., Berger, H., & Gulde, A. M. (2008). *Currency boards in retrospect and prospect*. MIT Press.

Zafiroski, J. (2018). *Monetary law*. University textbook (in Macedonian).

CHAPTER 7

Dependent Monetary Regimes in Post-Communist Balkan Periphery: Unilateral Euroization in Montenegro and Kosovo

Abstract In this chapter, we briefly present the discussion on the official euroization of dependent capitalisms from the former socialist bloc. We are focusing mainly on unilateral euroizations in Montenegro and Kosovo. The history of the change of monetary regimes in both countries has been reconstructed within the framework of the theory of dependent monetary regimes, presented in the previous chapters and applied to the introduction of Currency boards in Bulgaria and Bosnia and Herzegovina. Compared to Currency boards, the subordination of euroization and the dependence of the monetary regime on the leading monetary centre is significantly stronger, and euroization is entirely imposed by external actors and serves their interests. Despite the lack of nationally issued money, there are opportunities to pursue a limited discretionary monetary policy.

Keywords Montenegro · Kosovo · Euroization · Lender of last resort (LOLR) · Seigniorage · Deutsche Mark (DM)

E. Magnin and N. Nenovsky, *Diversity of Capitalism in Central and Eastern Europe*, https://doi.org/10.1007/978-3-031-04950-7_7

Introduction

In this chapter, we will focus on two other political entities that emerged after the break-up of the SFR Yugoslavia and unilaterally adopted the Deutsche Mark (and later the Euro)—Kosovo and Montenegro. Before that, we will note the following important but already forgotten fact. Following the decision to enlarge the European Union to the former socialist countries, as well as the transition to a single currency, the idea of a coordinated euroization of the entire former Eastern bloc, including the Balkans, has become widespread and met significant supporters.

We will point out the publications of the influential organization CEPS (CEPS, 1999; Gros, 1999).[1] The name of Romano Prodi, former President of the European Commission from 1999 to 2004, stands out among authors of CEPS reports. In CEPS reports, the idea of a formal and EU-ECB-coordinated comprehensive euroization of Western Balkans, or the Balkans in general, has been widely discussed and even technically considered. In this project, the transition from a Deutsche Mark-based Currency board (later Euro-based) to the introduction of the euro as national currency was a logical step in the general framework of the dependent monetary regime. Thus, according to CEPS report:

> Exploit new potential for wider euro, both for economic value and symbol for inclusion in modern Europe. Euro-based currency board regimes already possible. Full euroization for 1.1.2003 with budget compensation for loss of seigniorage for New Associate members. (CEPS, 1999, 3)

> Another key advantage of a currency board (followed by full euroisation) would be its systemic impact in transforming the political economy inside the country, and thus the chances of healthy economic growth. [...] For some countries in the region full euroization might be preferable to a mere currency board basically because of the full credibility it provides and because it allows considerable savings of foreign exchange reserves. However, for the practical reasons mentioned full euroisation would be difficult to implement quickly. Hence it might be best to start with a currency board to the euro at 1 (local currency): 1 (euro) as quickly as possible. This could then be transformed into full euroisation without much effort in 2002. (Gros, 1999, 4, 5)

[1] For a general survey on the region see Avramovic (1995), Coats and Skreb (2001), Barisitz (2007), Nenovsky (2009), Nenovsky and Villieu (2011) and Grittersovà (2014).

This intention for EU-coordinated euroization of the Balkans was quickly forgotten and a shift to unilateral euroization proposals took place. In 1999–2001, a discussion about unilateral euroization was held in Bulgaria.[2] In general, the majority of Bulgarian economists were sceptical about unilateral euroization. This was also determined by the negative position of European institutions towards euroization, which was accepted at that time. However, the first in-depth theoretical and empirical analysis of unilateral euroization was made in the study by Andrzej Bratkowski and Jacek Rostowski "*Unilateral Adoption of the Euro by EU Applicant Countries: The Macroeconomic Aspects (2001)*" (see also, Rostowski, 2002; Nuti, 2002).

Let us now consider *Montenegro* which became a pioneer in euroization in 1999 and a model for Kosovo to follow. It is interesting to note that Montenegro euroization was implemented, despite the official negative position of the EU and ECB on this regime.

Euroization in Montenegro

The decision for the separation of Montenegro from Yugoslavia, the last republic remaining in the Federation (from 28 April 1992 only Serbia and Montenegro remain in Yugoslavia), was not only accompanied but also implemented mainly by leaving the Yugoslavian Dinar zone.[3] As a result of the civil war, hyperinflation (and increased dinar printing), as well as the declining remittances that Montenegro received within the Federation in 1998/1999, the economic situation rapidly deteriorated. Local elites and their leader Milo Djukanovic steered towards economic and political independence, although the large part of the population was connected to Serbia (Dajkovic, 2001).

The Deutsche Mark was preferred by the population (holding five times more marks than dinars) and increasingly used as official currency. This spontaneous markization was later put forward as an argument that

[2] In support for euroization, as a next radical step toward monetary dependence after the CBA introduction, see the book "*From lev to euro. What's the best way?*" co-authored by Nikolay Nenovsky, Kalin Hristov and Boris Petrov (2001).

[3] It should be noted that within the federation with Serbia, the Central Bank of Montenegro completely lost its independence, in 1993. This was even a step back from the federal banking structure that existed in the former Yugoslavia, when for a certain period Montenegro had nominally a Central Bank (from 1972/1977 to 1993). For Yugoslavia see Lahiri (1991), Avramovic (1995), Jovic (2001) and Mitrović (2009).

seigniorage did not play a decisive role in the choice of a monetary regime. The decision to officially introduce the mark is also geopolitical in nature—it was imposed from outside, Germany in particular. The US authorities kept in step with that development, of which they were possibly among the initiators:

> The American emissary Mr Robert Gelbard, in his testimony before the United States Senate Foreign Relations Committee in 2000, described such a regime and the policy of that time as the guiding light for the rest of the region. (Fabris, 2015, 15)

One of the most active promoters of dollarization, Senator Connie Mack, eloquently formulated an idea for a mass official dollarization of a number of countries as follows:

> It has been said that money is coined liberty. Money gives people freedom of choice, freedom to innovate, freedom to enjoy the fruit of their labours. An untrustworthy currency is a kind of robbery. By limiting the usefulness of money, it limits choice, innovation, and investment. The US is fortunate to have a currency with one of the best long-term records in the world. We now have the opportunity to share the stability of the dollar with other countries, to our benefit and theirs. The benefits will be measured not just in terms of GDP, but in terms of fulfilling human potential. The accumulation of wealth that a trustworthy currency permits enables children to have better educations, families to take out longer-term mortgages for home ownership, and retirees' safety for their accumulated savings. By taking leadership on official dollarization, the US can advance prosperity and liberty the world over. (Mack, 2000, 69)

The steps for markization in Montenegro were the following: in early November 1999, a decision was made that the Deutsche Mark should be in circulation in parallel with the dinar, at a floating exchange rate. It is not certain whether it was coordinated or directly imposed by Germany and the Bundesbank (the facts and technical details are described in Schobert [2001, 2003]).[4] From November 1999 to November 2000, it circulated

[4] Particularly in Fabris et al. (2004), Fabris (2015), and Fabris and Galic (2016). See also Bogetić (2000), Bogetić and Hanke (2000), Hanke (1996/1997, 2002) and, for a general picture on euroization, see Scheiber and Stix (2009), OeN (2015) and Windischbauer (2016).

in parallel with the dinar. The government began to pay salaries in marks. The budget began to be formed in marks and taxes were paid in marks or in dinars at the exchange rate of the day.

Very quickly, the floating exchange rate eliminated the dinar altogether and, according to Franziska Schobert, in the middle of 2000 the dinar almost disappeared from circulation. In the period of parallel circulation, the monetary system was managed by a transitional monetary institution called Monetary Council, and in November, the new law on the Central Bank was adopted (Fabris, 2009, 15). The latter started operations from March 2001.[5] From January 2001, the Deutsche Mark became the only legal tender, and since March 2002, it has been replaced by the Euro.

Paradoxically, euroization seems at first sight to enable monetary policy. Montenegro's system, unlike that of Kosovo (cf. below), allowed some use of different monetary policy instruments. Apart from required reserves, from 2011 the CBCG (Central Bank of Montenegro) adopted OMO regulation in two forms: (i) permanent OM transactions and (ii) Repo transactions. Besides, in case of liquidity problems, CBCG can grant three types of loans: (i) intraday liquidity loan, (ii) overnight loan and (iii) short-term liquidity loan (maximum twice for three months). Of course, all operations are against collateral and with progressively rising interest rates.

In certain extreme cases, it may also perform LOLR functions. Again, under strict collateral requirements and at an interest rate of 3% above the ECB base rate.[6] From 2018/2019, the CBCG, following the policy of the ECB, began to also actively use macroprudential regulation as: different types of capital buffers (countercyclical, systemic risk, other systemically important institution), leverage and liquidity coverage ratio, etc. In the absence of a domestic LOLR, the need for a protective external LOLR is especially evident in a crisis. Therefore, in August 2020, during the pandemics, CBCG concluded two safety repo lines with the BIS and the ECB.

[5] In 2007, Montenegro's new constitution was adopted. This led to a change in the law on the Central Bank, which took on new CB functions in 2010, making it responsible for financial stability.

[6] The Central Bank also conducts auctions for 6 months T-bills issued by the government. For example, in 2000, 8 auctions were held, and in some of them, the volumes offered were significantly higher than the bids, and respectively, interest rates were higher than those in the euro area (about 1%). There is no reference rate because of the monetary policy regime.

Curiously, the case in point in Montenegro is a monetary policy in euro; that is, the money supply and its structure can be changed within certain boundaries (CBCG, 2015). In euroized country, money supply is a direct result of the balance of payments dynamics. It mostly relies on foreign capital, emigrants' transfers (remittances) and official aid from IFIs. Trade flows, though important, such as tourism receipts for Montenegro, are not a determining factor.

After the successful initial period for the Montenegrin economy, in recent years there has been a deterioration in public finances, as well as attempts to stabilize them. On the eve of the pandemic, public debt was within the range of 65 to 75% of GDP, and the deficit from (−8.3%) in 2015 reached (−2.0%) in 2019. The pandemic reversed the trend. Debt and deficit inevitably increased; unemployment spreads, and the country is in deflation, following the trends in the euro area.[7]

The case of Montenegro is also interesting in that it raises the important issue of seigniorage as a motive for preserving national money and for choosing CBA over euroization. In a series of empirical studies, Franziska Schobert has shown that its importance is overstated both in Montenegro and on the Balkans, as well as in the CEE countries (see Schobert, 2001, 2002, 2003) (Table 7.1).

Euroization in Kosovo

Taking a look at the recent monetary history of Kosovo, we can immediately observe that the change of the monetary regime was directly devised by external forces (United Nations Interim Administration Mission in Kosovo (UNMIK), the US Treasury, IMF, NATO, EU, etc.). The start was given after recognition by Western powers of the self-proclaimed Republic of Kosovo in May 1992 in violation of UN norms.

Unlike Bosnia and Herzegovina, initially Kosovo had almost no national political structures or elements of statehood (no formal government); chaos and criminal activity of all kinds reigned.[8] The interim economic and financial administration in Kosovo was carried out by

[7] See EC for details (2020, 14–17). In September 2020, S&P reaffirmed its B+/B rating and negative outlook.

[8] It is worth noting that accusations of corruption have not spared the Central Bank either, even years later. In 2010, the Governor of the Central Bank was accused of corruption (and later acquitted).

Table 7.1 Kosovo and Montenegro: Main macroeconomic indicators (2000–2019)

	2000	*2005*	*2010*	*2015*	*2019*
Economic growth, %, y/y change					
Kosovo	na	6,03	3,31	4,10	4,17
Montenegro	3,10	4,18	2,73	3,39	4,06
Inflation, consumer prices (annual %)					
Kosovo	na	−1,39	3,48	−0,54	2,68
Montenegro	na	na	0,65	1,55	0,37
Debt/GDP, %					
Kosovo	na	na	6,22	13,07	17,46
Montenegro	na	42,70	42,00	63,30	65,00
Government deficit (% of GDP)					
Kosovo	2,24	−3,07	−2,60	−1,30	−0,30
Montenegro	na	−1,41	−4,87	−5,96	−2,40
Deposit interest rate (%)					
Kosovo	na	2,89	3,70	0,90	na
Montenegro	na	4,84	3,70	1,46	0,46
Lending interest rate (%)					
Kosovo	na	14,42	14,37	8,32	na
Montenegro	na	12,41	9,53	8,93	6,18
FDI, net inflows (% of GDP)					
Kosovo	na	3,65	8,40	5,33	3,84
Montenegro	na	na	18,30	17,27	8,35
Foreign reserves/GDP (constant 2010 US$)					
Kosovo	na	na	13,94	11,29	12,06
Montenegro	na	na	13,42	15,04	28,62
Corporate tax rate, %					
Kosovo	na	na	na	10,00	10,00
Montenegro	na	9,00	9,00	9,00	9,00
Net Domestic Credit, %, y/y					
Kosovo	na	8,85	15,75	33,85	50,81
Montenegro	na	15,93	87,59	91,22	78,71
Foreign bank assets/total assets					
Kosovo	na	na	na	na	na
Montenegro	na	23,0	100,0	na	na
Minimum wages, USD					
Kosovo	na	na	na	na	na
Montenegro	na	na	na	349,70	329,80

Sources World Bank, Trading Economics, Global Economy, Country Economy

foreign entities ("external government"), most notably UNMIK, which was assigned to this task by UN Resolution 1244 of 10 June 1999. At this initial point, the population and businesses widely used the Deutsche Mark. Similarly to Bosnia and Herzegovina, the payment system of the area was located in Belgrade (i.e. SDKK payment bureau).[9]

In 1999/2001, UNMIK set up the Banking and Payments Authority of Kosovo (BPAK), and in 2006, it was transformed into Central Banking Authority of Kosovo (CBAK). After the ceasefire in 1998, the Deutsche Mark was declared a legal tender, initially alongside with the Serbian Dinar, and subsequently on its own (this happened on 2 September 1999). During the changeover from the Deutsche Mark to the Euro, about 1 million marks were exchanged in cash (for details see BPAK, 2002). In the beginning, the governing bodies of monetary authorities were mostly staffed by foreigners (Softić, 2017).

The Central Bank of the Republic of Kosovo (CBRK), as a sovereign body, was established in 2008. Unlike the Central Bank of Bosnia and Herzegovina, here the Central Bank does not precede euroization (adoption of the mark and the euro as national money), but follows it and legitimizes it. The CBRK started to operate under an euroization regime, with the main goal of creating security for market participants and reducing the overall risk level. The aim was to attract FDI and to guarantee Albanians security in their remittances. The amounts of these remittances reached 25–30% of GDP[10] (see also Fig. 5.4 in Chapter 5). Unlike in the case of Bulgaria and Bosnia and Herzegovina, in Kosovo the mark and later the euro were imposed entirely from outside, almost without the participation of local actors. The main task of the CBRK and the euroization was to create an efficient market economy.

> CBRK main goals are outlined as following: "(1) The primary objective of the Central Bank shall be to foster and to maintain a stable financial system, including a safe, sound and efficient payment system. (2) An additional objective of the Central Bank, which is subordinated to the primary objective of the Central Bank, is to contribute to achieving and maintaining domestic price stability. (3) Without prejudice to attainment of these two objectives, the Central Bank shall support the general economic policies

[9] It was not until 2001 that an independent Interbank Clearing System was created, and in 2007, it expanded into the Electronic Interbank Clearing System (EICS).

[10] Winkler et al. (2004, 41).

> of the Government. (4) The Central Bank shall act in accordance with the principle of an open market economy with free competition, favouring an efficient allocation of resources". (CBRK, Law on the Central bank of Republic of Kosovo 03/L209, 2010)

The second leading motive, according to all participants, was to overcome the "inflationary, financial trauma". This trauma was extremely deep, because being part of Yugoslavia, Kosovo experienced severe hyperinflation. We will quote an interesting study of Emina Abuannab, in which she presents interviews with leading political figures:

> We rely greatly on remittances as a state. Our people were used to keeping DM, pounds and USD under the mattress for decades as a safety net shall there be another hyperinflation. Making DM and Euro official helped them take the money out from under the mattress and transfer some of that confidence into our institutions. Restoring or rebuilding the use of a former currency was not even an option. (Interview 1) (Abuannab, 2019, 61)

CBRK takes care mainly of foreign reserve management, of banking regulations and the payment system, and of the management of government finances (Coats, 2007; NBK, 2015). It does not perform LOLR functions. According to evidence:

> When asked about the LLR function, representative from the CBRK answer carefully: "The CBRK is not a lender of last resort and we never applied this policy" (Interview 2). (Abuannab, 2019, 57)

In Kosovo, there exist limited monetary instruments, the so-called fixed deposits and Emergency Liquidity Assistance. Due to the euroization of the country, interest rates are almost the same as in the euro area (they are called "Kosovo's ECB interest rate"). In recent years, the bank has been actively developing supervisory and regulatory activities, which within certain limits can play the role of monetary policy.

Concluding Remarks

The two extremely static and externally dependent monetary regimes presented here and in the previous chapter, Currency board and euroization, could be considered as exceptions, rather than being indicative of the overall developments on the Balkans.[11] Still, the peculiar monetary regimes in these four countries are no exception: they are rather a manifestation of a general dynamics, observable, although in a milder form, in other Balkan countries, which are at different phases and forms of the same dynamics of crony transition and monetary dependence. As for the Balkans, they run completely or almost completely dependent monetary regimes, i.e. extreme forms of fixed and quasi-fixed exchange rates, as well as high coverage of the monetary base (even in cases where they are not Currency boards).[12] Even when this is not officially declared, central banks in Balkan countries pursue a conservative monetary policy that mimics CBA principles. As far as the exchange rate regime is concerned, empirical evidence shows that the exchange rate is the main monetary anchor of these countries with equilibria occurring through it and to a much lesser extent through changes in foreign exchange reserves (Frömmel & Schobert, 2006).[13]

The above four examples of dependent monetary regimes have all the characteristics that we have set out in previous chapters and which fit into the theory of dependent capitalism. Their implementation is accompanied by a political, economic, military and geopolitical crisis, and aims to stabilize the country's monetary and financial system for the needed foreign investments and foreign banks. Considering the structural economic and political constraints of the Balkan countries, the functioning of dependent monetary regimes can be considered successful both within the short term—stabilization plan—and in terms of creating conditions for future economic development. But the latter is related to the issue of technological growth of national productions and to a movement towards higher technological levels in international value chains.

From the standpoint of the experience gained over the last 20 years, some important conditions for the successful functioning of dependent monetary regimes can be highlighted. Some of them were partially

[11] It can be argued that these four countries are small and micro in population (Bulgaria 7 million, Bosnia and Herzegovina 3.3 million, Kosovo about 1.8 million and Montenegro 600 thousand), with the larger ones adopting/operating CBAs and the smaller ones being euroized, respectively. Various stages in the evolution of monetary regimes and banking systems on the Balkans have been the subject of a number of studies. See in particular Šević (2002) and Fullani (2009).

[12] See IMF (2015) and Vujčić (2004).

[13] See Frömmel et al. (2011).

presumed, while others were not foreseen at all at the beginning. We will mention three of them:

First, dependent monetary regimes can only exist in a specific institutional environment that is characteristic of dependent capitalism in general. Of foremost significance are conservative public finances and a flexible labour market, which do not threaten the existence of the orthodox monetary regime, both in terms of raising public debt and through the mechanism of loss of competitiveness through the exchange rate. Second, there must be a steady and predictable inflow of FDI and capital portfolios to offset negative current account balances. In the case of Bulgaria, for example, different European funds played a significant role. Obviously, the domestic political will to preserve the regime is crucial.

Second, these regimes must find alternative mechanisms to manage the vulnerability that arises from the pro-cyclicality of credit growth and the dominant presence of foreign banks and their branches, i.e. the growth of private household and corporate debt. In the extreme forms of dependent monetary regimes, monetary instruments for controlling the pro-cyclicality of credit, as well as the sharp withdrawals of bank capital in case of a crisis, are extremely limited. However, practice has shown that the lack of monetary policy can be successfully replaced by well-designed banking and credit regulations.

Third, and perhaps the most important thing that almost no one noted when introducing these dependent regimes, was the problem of the stability of the anchor itself, the stability and prospects for the area and the currency against which the Balkan countries pegged themselves. In fact, the pattern is simple and easy to understand. When the anchor area develops well and transfers capital to the periphery, things go well for the periphery in general. However, when the zone is in crisis, the periphery fully takes on its problems since it does not have its own mechanisms for balancing and resistance. In certain situations, the lack of or limited LOLR leads to the emergence of substitutes: external LOLR, various types of protective swaps, etc. The global crisis, as well as today's pandemic, has clearly shown this need.

Dependent monetary regimes and dependent capitalism in general, which may be successful under certain conditions in peripheral countries, have extremely limited mechanisms of response to crises and to rare and unpredictable events. The pandemic, which began in early 2020 and is still going on today, provides us with empirical material for some initial observations and summaries on the sustainability and quality of dependent monetary regimes. To conclude this book, we will look at some of them.

References

Abuannab, E. (2019). *Structural constraints and choice in monetary policy regime design: Bosnia and Kosovo in comparative perspective*. İhsan Doğramacı Bilkent University.

Avramovic, D. (1995). *Reconstruction of the monetary system and economic recovery of Yugoslavia, analytical framework, results and problems* (WIIW Research Reports, N° 216).

BPAK (Banking and Payment Authority of Kosovo). (2002). *2002 annual report*. Prishtina. https://bqk-kos.org/repository/docs/2010/Annual%20Report%2002.pdf

Barisitz, S. (2007). Exchange rate arrangements and monetary policy in Southeastern Europe: An update (2004–2007). *OeNB Focus on European Economic Integration, 2*(7), 78–99.

Bogetić, Ž. (2000). Official dollarization: Current experiences and issues. *Cato Journal, 20*(2), 179–213.

Bogetić, Ž., & Hanke, S. (1999). *Projekat valutnog odbora za Crnu Goru – Crnogorska marka*, Radio Antena M i Mermont.

Bratkowski, A., & Rostowski, J. (2001). Unilateral adoption of the Euro by EU applicant countries: The macroeconomic aspects. In L. Orlowski (Ed.), *Transition and growth in Post-Communist countries: The 10 year experience* (pp. 125–147). Edward Elgar Publishing.

CBCG. (2020a, December). *Macroprudential measures related to retail banking loans, and measures to preserve financial stability*. Central Bank of Montenegro. https://www.cbcg.me/en

CBCG. (2020b, December). *Decision on open market operation, on credit operations*. Central Bank of Montenegro. https://www.cbcg.me/en

CBCG. (2018). *Macroprudential policy framework*. Central Bank of Montenegro.

CBCG. (2015). *CBCG monetary policy instruments*. Central Bank of Montenegro.

CBRK (2010). *Law on the Central Bank of Republic of Kosovo*. https://www.bqk-kos.org/repository/docs/2010/Ligji%20per%20BQK-ne%20(anglisht).pdf.

CBRK. (2015). *Godišnji izveštaj 2014*. Centralna Banka Republike Kosova.

CEPS. (1999). *A system for Post-War South-East Europe (Plan for reconstruction, openness, development and integration)* (Centre for European Policy Studies WP N° 131).

Coats, W. (2007). *Monetary policy issues in post conflict economies*. New York University's Center on International Cooperation (J. K. Boyce & M. O'Donnell, Eds.). Rienner. http://works.bepress.com/cgi/viewcontent.cgi?article=1008&context=warren_coats

Coats, W., & Skreb, M. (2001). Central banking in transition: An overview of main ten years after, Revue d'économie financière. In Special Issue: *Ten Years of transformation in Eastern European countries. Achievements and challenges* (pp. 265–286). AEF.

Cohen, B. (1998). *The geography of money*. Cornel University Press.

Dajkovic, A. (2001). *A «Model» for the Balkans*. https://zcomm.org/zmagazine/a-model-for-the-balkans-by-alex-n-dajkovic/

EC. (2020). *EU candidate countries' & potential candidates' Economic Quarterly, 3rd Quarter 2020* (European Commission Technical Paper N° 044).

Fabris, N., Vukajlovic-Grba, D., Radunović, T., Janković, H. (2004). *Economic policy in dollarized economies with a special review of Montenegro* (WP N°1). The Central Bank of Montenegro.

Fabris, N. (2009). Implications of dollarization with special overview of Montenegro. In K. Ralf & A. Socic (Eds.), *Transformations monétaires et financières dans les pays d'Europe centrale et orientale* (pp. 3–30), Les Cahiers de Recherche, ESCE, N°1.

Fabris, N. (2015). The history of money in Montenegro. *Journal of Central Banking Theory and Practice, 4*(1), 5–18.

Fabris, N., & Galic, J. (2016, January). *Comparative analysis of monetary policy arrangements: Examples of Serbia, Macedonia and Montenegro*. Paper presented at BALKINT Conference, Belgrade.

Frömmel, M., Schobert, F., Garabedian, G. (2011). Monetary policy rules in Central and Eastern European Countries: Does the exchange rate matter?, *Journal of Macroeconomics, 33*(4): 807–818

Frömmel, M., & Schobert, F. (2006). Exchange rate regimes in Central and East European Countries: Deeds vs. words. *Journal of Comparative Economics, 34*(3), 467–483.

Fullani, A. (Ed.). (2009). *Monetary policy strategies for small economies*. Bank of Albania.

Gilbert, A., & Mujanović, J. (2015). Dayton at twenty: Towards new politics in Bosnia-Herzegovina. *Southeast European and Black Sea Studies, 15*(4), 605–610.

Grittersovà, J. (2014). Exchange rates in transition economies. In Th. Oatley (Ed.), *The international political economy of the international monetary and financial system*. Edward Elgar.

Gros, D. (1999). *An economic system for Post-War South-East Europe* (Centre for European Policy Studies WP N° 131 [a companion paper])

Hanke, S. H. (1996/1997). A field report from Sarajevo and Pale. *Central Banking, 7*(3), 36–40.
Hanke, S. (2002). On dollarization and currency boards: Error and deception. *Policy Reform, 5*(4), 203–222.
IMF. (2020). *Annual report on exchange arrangements and exchange restrictions 2019.* IMF.
IMF. (2015). *The Western Balkans: 15 years of economic transition.* Regional Economic Issues Special Report, IMF Washington.
Joireman, S. (2016). External conditionalities and institutional change: Constructing constituencies for the rule of law in Kosovo. *East European Politics and Societies, 30*(2), 315–331.
Jovic, D. (2001). The disintegration of Yugoslavia: A critical review of explanatory approaches. *European Journal of Social Theory, 4*(1), 101–120.
Lahiri, A. (1991). *Money and inflation in Yugoslavia* (IMF Working Paper N° 91/50).
Mack, C. (2000). Why the US should encourage dollarization. *Central Banking, 11*(1), 63–69.
Mitrović, L. (2009). *Tranzicija u periferni kapitalizam: (ogledi iz sociologije globalnih regionalnih promena).* Inst. za Političke Studije.
MONET. (2001). *Montenegro economic trends.* ISSP-CEPS, Podgorica, Montenegro.
National Bank of Serbia (NBS). (2015, March). *Report on the Dinarization of the Serbian Financial System.* National Bank of Serbia.
Nenovsky, N. (2009). *Monetary regimes in Post-Communist countries: Some long-term reflections* (Working Paper No.2). Agency for Economic Analysis and Forecasting.
Nenovsky, N., & Villieu, P. (2011). EU enlargement and monetary regimes from the insurance model perspectives. *Post-Communist Economies, 23*(4), 433–447.
Nuti, D. (2002). Costs and benefits of unilateral euroisation in central eastern Europe. *Economics of Transition, 10*, 419–444.
OeN. (2015). *The Euro in Central, Eastern and South-eastern Europe.* Euro Survey. Austrian Central Bank.
Scheiber, T., & Stix, H. (2009). *Euroization in Central, Eastern and South-eastern Europe—New evidence on its extent and some evidence on its causes* (Working Paper No.159). Oesterreichische Nationalbank.
Rostowski, J. (2002). Why unilateral Euroization makes sense for (some) Applicant countries. In M. Dabrowski, B. Slay, & J. Neneman (Eds.), *Beyond transition: Development perspectives and dilemmas* (pp. 74–90). Ashgate.
Roaf, J., Ayoyan, R., Joshi, B., & Krogulski, K. (Eds.). (2014). *25 Years of transition. Post-Communist Europe and the IMF (Special report).* International Monetary Fund.

Schobert, F. (2003). *Die unilaterale Einführungeiner Fremdwährung. Währungswahl, Seigniorage und Zinsprämieneffekte in mittel- undosteuropäischen Ländern,* Schriftenreihe volkswirtschaftliche Forschungsergebnisse. Verlag Dr. Kovac.

Schobert, F. (2001). The change-over to the Euro in Montenegro: Causes and Consequences. *Ifo Studien, Zeitschrift Für Empirische Wirtschaftsforschung, 47*(3), 283–309.

Schobert, F. (2002). *Seigniorage: An argument for a national currency?* (CEPS Research Report, N° 28).

Šević, Ž (Ed.). (2002). *Banking reforms in South-East Europe.* Edward Elgar.

Softić, S. (Ed). (2017). *Central Bank of Bosnia and Herzegovina. 20 years of stability, 1997–2017.* Central Bank of Bosnia and Herzegovina, Sarajevo.

Vujčić, B. (2004). Euro adoption: Views from the third row. *Comparative Economic Studies, 46*(1), 159–176.

Windischbauer, U. (2016). *Strengthening the role of local currencies in EU candidate and potential candidate countries* (ECB Occasional Paper N° 170).

Winkler, A., Mazzafero, F., Nerkich, H., & Thimann, C. (2004). *Official Dollarisation/Euroisation: Motives, features and policy implications of current cases* (ECB Occasional Paper Series N° 11). European Central Bank.

PART III

Conclusion

CHAPTER 8

Concluding Remarks: Dependent Monetary Regimes During the Pandemics

Abstract This chapter first summarizes the main results unveiled throughout the pages of this book. To name but a few: the exceptional development of the field of Comparative Capitalism since the 1990s, especially regarding the application to CEE countries (Balkans included), and the dialogue between VoC and RT; the emergence of a new family of capitalisms in post-socialist Central and Eastern Europe, dependent capitalism; the revival of dependency theories in a new theoretical and historical context; the evidence of dependent monetary regimes in the Balkans complementary to other institutional forms constituting the model, etc. Secondly, it shows how dependent monetary regimes in the countries studied have faced the COVID-19 crisis and highlights some of the first lessons to be learned. Finally, it presents some avenues for future research.

Keywords Pandemics · Central bank swaps · Covid 19 crisis · Lock-in · Banking regulatory measures · Crisis measures (monetary Fiscal Regulatory) · Stimulus (monetary Fiscal)

E. Magnin and N. Nenovsky, *Diversity of Capitalism in Central and Eastern Europe*, https://doi.org/10.1007/978-3-031-04950-7_8

Main Points of the Book

Since the 1990s, research on comparing models of capitalism throughout the world has developed considerably. Comparative Capitalism (CC) has become a major issue as it brings to the fore societal choices and national socio-economic compromises. The "transition to a market economy" in the CEECs is not alien to the development of this literature, as it raised the question of the type of capitalism likely to emerge as a result of the institutional, economic and political transformations implemented. Moreover, the CEE countries have become a privileged field of application for the main approaches constituting CC. However, the development of the latter meets other challenges and other transitions, beyond the changes made in the CEE countries, to which this book is devoted. Besides the large number of studies highlighting the diversity of models on other continents (Asia, Latin America, Africa), the ecological transition, for example, brings new ideas. Different models of capitalism mean different ways of implementing this transition, some of which may prove more successful than others. Similarly, the digital transition and the COVID-19 pandemic have given a central role to platform capitalism, which is likely to have an impact on the different national configurations (Boyer, 2020).

The CEE systemic transformation put the emphasis on the two main approaches found in CC literature: the VoC approach and the "diversity of capitalism" derived from the theory of *Régulation (RT)*. With a few exceptions, most of the work in this field can be related in some way to one of the above approaches (Chapter 2). By bringing to light the vulnerabilities of CEE countries, the 2008 financial crisis revealed the emergence of a dependent model of capitalism with differentiated national forms. While dependent capitalism belongs originally to the VoC tradition, especially since Nölke and Vligenthart's work on dependent market economies (DMEs), the other approach has been favoured in this book by transposing DMEs analysis into the RT framework. Two main reasons explain this choice. On the one hand, the limits of the VoC framework, which may be considered as firm-centred and a-historical, constrain the analysis in terms of DMEs, while this is not the case with RT. On the other hand, RT is a more comprehensive theory of capitalism and its dynamics (growth and crises), which introduces the concept of institutional hierarchy in addition to institutional complementarity (also included in VoC). However, like the VoC approach, RT was initially built on the basis of developed Western economies and may appear less suited to emerging economies.

In a nutshell, dependent capitalism can be defined as an economic model which relies on foreign capital (mainly FDIs, bank credits or sometimes remittances) to sustain growth and capital accumulation. The latter are therefore "dependent" on decisions taken by actors outside the countries concerned, such as MNCs. In Central and Eastern Europe, this situation is consistent with the integration of these economies into Western European (especially German) value chains. Dependent capitalism is characterized by specific institutional arrangements, which demonstrate complementarity relationships, thereby ensuring the stability of the model over time. Within the VoC approach, a comparative advantage is identified in the production of relatively complex and durable consumer goods. In the RT framework, it is also possible to identify a form of institutional hierarchy and an outward-oriented accumulation regime, sustained by the hierarchized fundamental institutional forms that characterize it (Chapter 3).

The concept of dependence refers to the Marxist theories of the 1960s–1970s in Latin America, but it is here revisited in a very different theoretical and historical context.[1] In particular, it allows us to go beyond the Western-centred character of comparative capitalism, while emphasizing the asymmetrical relations of dependence between models of capitalism in the world. From this point of view, dependence is not synonymous with interdependence, as an easy and misleading criticism might suggest. Moreover, it moves away from the classic centre/periphery opposition, emphasizing political coalitions and power relations between national elites and external actors (MNCs, international organizations, EU) and the contradictory dynamics of dependence and development.

The emergence of dependent capitalism in Central and Eastern Europe (Balkans included) appears to be the path-dependent outcome of initial conditions ("perceived" legacy) and reforms implemented under international organizations and EU influences, and supported by political and economic elites. These transformations lead to the emergence of differentiated models of dependence, which are not mutually exclusive:

[1] It is not insignificant to note the influence of an economist from the European periphery, the Romanian Mihail Manoilescu (1891–1950) and his theory of protectionism, which has been proven to be one of the sources of Latin American structuralism and dependence theory (Love, 1996; Nenovsky & Torre, 2015, 2018).

dependence on FDI and exports, foreign debt and/or remittances from migrants. Despite its adverse effects, the 2008 financial crisis did not undermine the stability of dependent capitalism.

The monetary regime, one of RT's fundamental institutional forms, is a salient illustration of the dependent character of capitalism in Central and Eastern Europe (Balkans included). These countries' necessity to attract external capital in the context of the post-socialist transition led them to adopt different forms of dependent monetary regimes in line with those of the more developed (Western European) countries and in keeping with their interests, so as to ensure returns on capital and stability and to reassure foreign investors. Dependent monetary regimes constrain the economic monetary sovereignty of a country, both in its domestic dimension—monetary policy—and in terms of the exchange rate regime. Monetary and exchange rate policies passively follow the monetary and exchange rate policies of the country (or the currency area) chosen as an external anchor (see Chapter 4). In broader theoretical terms, the monetary dependence of certain countries is determined by the structural (albeit dynamic) hierarchy that exists between national currencies internationally. This hierarchy, in turn, reflects, in most cases, the economic and geopolitical hierarchy between countries and the role of their leading economic and financial groups. It is clear, for example, that countries with high global economic, trade and financial weight, whose money is sought after as international money, can finance their development in their own money at the expense of those countries whose money has only national and limited demand. The Balkan countries show some extreme forms of dependent monetary regimes, such as Currency boards in Bulgaria and Bosnia-Herzegovina or euroization in Kosovo and Montenegro (see Chapters 6and7). These institutional arrangements may nevertheless be appropriate and minimize losses and risks in situations of significant institutional change (such as transition) and/or weak states (Delteil, 2018).

More generally, dependent capitalism may, in some cases, not be a flawed model if dependence does not constrain development and lock the economy into a low-road trajectory. In order to avoid a lock-in, «domestic» investment in new technologies and education appear to be key variables. In this respect, European aid such as structural and cohesion policy, aimed at reducing regional disparities, could help overcome the constraints of dependence, replacing the role of the developmental state in Asia. The countries of Central and Eastern Europe seem a priori to be the most likely to upgrade their trajectory. However, in response to nationalist reactions in Hungary and Poland, partly fuelled by this situation of dependence, which they reject, voices are being raised to reconsider the European solidarity from which they benefit and which they need to overcome this situation.

The 2020 health crisis accelerates some transformations initiated in previous years, among others the development of platform capitalism, the return of the interventionist state or pressures on natural resources (Boyer, 2020). European fiscal and monetary policies have also made a U-turn by massively supporting the economies of the region. The question then arises as to whether the COVID-19 pandemic challenges or consolidates the developments observed in this book since the 1990s, especially with regard to the dependent monetary regime of the countries studied.

Dependent Monetary Regimes During the Pandemic

As we have seen so far, and especially in Chapter 4, Dependent Monetary Regimes have been accused of having limited capacity to respond to a systemic crisis in the short term, as well as difficulties mobilizing resources for longer-term development. The pandemic crisis that began in late 2019 represents an empirical test for the sustainability and effectiveness of DMRs. Without elaborated in detail the relationship between the pandemic and monetary regimes, we note the following points (see Fig. 8.1).

The pandemic crisis, now in its third year, is a specific, exogenously induced economic systemic crisis, manifested in a joint contraction of demand and supply.[2] The pandemic has posed a number of policy problems for public authorities, most notably the arbitrage between short- and long-term policy responses, and finding the right coordination between monetary, fiscal and regulatory policies (Boissay et al., 2020; English et al., 2021). This means (i) in the short term, providing liquidity to economic agents (small, medium and large businesses, households and banks). Bank regulations and fiscal packages (by increasing deficits and

[2] See some of the early reviews of the pandemic: Johns Hopkins Coronavirus Resource Center (2020), Eichenbaum et al. (2020) and IMF (2021a, b).

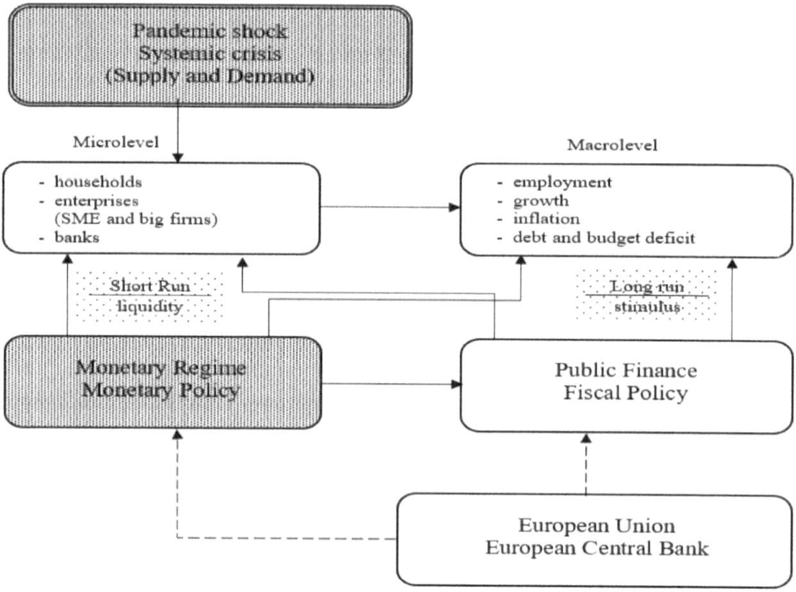

Fig. 8.1 Theoretical framework for understanding monetary regime during the pandemic (*Source* Sahling et al. [2021, p. 279])

debt) are also relevant here. And (ii) in the long run, conducting monetary policy and creating fiscal stimulus and programs aimed at restoring the economy and eventually setting new trajectories for long-term and sustainable growth.

It is evident from the known characteristics of DMRs that their capabilities are extremely limited. In the case of a DMR, the creation of a monetary base is entirely externally determined through the balance of payments. Central Bank cannot create liquidity by acquiring securities and conducting OMO, quantitative easing (QE), interest rate cuts, etc. DMRs set extremely restrictive limits on the government. The government cannot run deficits and accumulate debts because they become a threat to the fixed exchange rate (if Currency board) and to the banking system (if euroization). The dominant presence of foreign banks also increases the vulnerability of the DMR, because of possible capital flight within banking groups.[3] There are, of course, opportunities to have precautionary liquidity through Central Bank swaps and repos agreements.

Finally, it should also be noted that there is a hypothetical possibility that DMRs may prove to be more successful and efficient in the long run (higher growth and lower inflation), and that it is their conservatism that is the reason for this.

Turning to the response of monetary and fiscal authorities during the pandemic in the highly dependent monetary regimes of Bulgaria, Bosnia and Herzegovina, Montenegro and Kosovo, the following stylized facts could be mentioned.

First, the nature of the measures and the volumes of interventions by governments and central banks confirm the limited possibilities of these regimes. Second, under DMRs, there is no scope for influencing interest rates, for asset and debt purchases, for targeted lending operations and for expansion of the Central Bank's balance sheet in general. In some cases, changes in banks' reserve requirements are used, but this is rare. Third, fiscal intervention and stimulus packages are also modest in size compared to other countries in the Balkan region, which also follow closely the monetary policy of the centre (ECB), preserving to some extent elements of monetary independence. Fourthly, the limited national fiscal space is partly compensated by expected funds under various European programs (Bulgaria, for example, expects significant transfers under the EU Next Generation Programme, in addition to the current funds related to the COVID-19). Pre-accession and other types of aid are also being received by the other three countries.

Fifth, the countries under review mostly use supervisory and macro-regulatory interventions in relation to the banking sector. They are a kind of substitute for monetary policy. The latter include capital and liquidity relief for banks through changes in exposures and various buffers (especially easing of the countercyclical capital buffer), easing of provisioning and classifications, restriction of dividend payments, etc. Of course, administrative measures include the moratorium on lending, etc. The regulatory measures referred to broadly follow those taken by the monetary centre, in this case the ECB, and by the European banking authorities. Sixthly, since the LOLR function is absent in the DMR, in

[3] There were such moments in Bulgaria, after its entry into the Banking Union, but the BNB had taken preventive regulatory measures.

some cases precautionary bilateral swaps are concluded with the ECB (e.g. Bulgaria) or repo transactions with the ECB (e.g. Montenegro).

It should be noted, however, that, as in most countries in Europe, banks were highly liquid during the pandemic period in the four countries under consideration. Mostly, this is due to the fact that the banks are foreign batches and have access to funding from their parent banks, which in turn have access to ECB instruments and abundant QE liquidity. As a result, the overall level of credit has not contracted, but maintained its levels (unlike the dynamism of credit in the crisis that started in 2008). Also, banks have been making loan write-downs in anticipation of a rise in non-performing loans following the suspension of the moratorium and the emergence of business and household defaults.

It is necessary to take into account that all four countries are attached to an area whose Central Bank has pursued during the pandemic an extremely expansionary monetary policy (negative interest rates, QE, etc.). ECB policy in different forms influences monetary processes in the countries under consideration. Finally, it is worth noting that the DMR have generally proved resilient to the systemic pandemic shock, and early statistics show a rapid recovery of these economies (Bykova, 2021). The future will show to what extent these regimes can ensure a long-term growth and control inflation processes. So far, they have withstood the systemic shock.

Possible Future Research

In the years to come, studying the evolution of dependent capitalism in Central and Eastern Europe and the Balkans will allow us to assess, on the one hand, whether the model is sustainable over time, and, on the other hand, whether it is able to reconcile dependence and economic catching-up by increasing the technological content of production and the added value generated on the national territory, or, on the contrary, whether it is locked into a low-road trajectory. In this respect, it would certainly be interesting to consider the "performance" of the model, based on a broad definition of performance including economic, social and environmental criteria. As pointed out several times in the book, the model's institutional configuration and performance are likely to evolve differently depending on the countries and geographical areas concerned (Central and Eastern Europe, Baltic countries, Balkans). Among various possible scenarios, the return of the state in many countries since 2010 (Boyer,

2020), for economic reasons (demand for state protection accentuated by the 2008 financial crisis and then by the COVID-19 pandemic) and political considerations (populism, defence of national identity), could lead dependent countries and their elites to adopt a form of state capitalism, if only because of a rejection of external dependence, as evidenced by nationalist temptations in Hungary and Poland. However, this scenario must be qualified given the size of the country and the domestic market; small countries can hardly afford not to be open to foreign trade and foreign investment.

Dependent monetary regime, a key element in the institutional structure of dependent capitalism, is a promising research topic, in both theoretical and empirical, applied terms. From a theoretical perspective, it is important to study in detail the mechanisms of monetary dependence, and that in microeconomic and behavioural terms. This means how individuals, households, enterprises, banks and governments are placed in the constraint of a dependent monetary regime, and how they adapt to it through their behaviour and different strategies. In this regard, it is also interesting to investigate the distributive and redistributive role of the dependent monetary regime, who gains and who loses from it, and how consensus is reached over the institutional imposition of such a regime (i.e. the role of interests, ideas, power, etc.) (Nenovsky & Rizopoulos, 2003, 2004).

It is also interesting to explore in more depth the differences in dependent monetary regimes and the specificities in the manifestation of monetary dependence (types of Currency boards, types of dollarization, different constructions of monetary unions, etc.). Of course, a fundamental theoretical analysis within a pure theory of money is important in itself, i.e. to conceptualize the notion of dependence, which for the time being remains at the level of monetary regime and monetary system. The legal and economic dimensions of dependence also need to be more clearly delineated (e.g. the concept of sovereignty). The rapid proliferation of digital currency (in decentralized or centralized form) is also changing the debate on monetary dependence (e.g. the adoption of bitcoin as official money in dollarized Ecuador, or the Central Bank digital currency wars).

A historical perspective in examining monetary regimes in the periphery of the world economy would also yield interesting conclusions.

A first look at the history of the monetary regimes of the Balkan countries, from the nineteenth century to the present, presented in Magnin and Nenovsky (2022), shows the existence of a long-term, albeit cyclical, dependence of the region's monetary systems and regimes. It is interesting to note, for example, that within the socialist period, the monetary regimes of the small socialist countries were attached to the Soviet monetary zone (a kind of "dependent socialism"?), while such relatively independent countries as Yugoslavia followed the monetary anchor of the West (USA, subsequently Germany).

References

Boissay, F., Rees, D., & Rungcharoenkitkul, P. (2020). *Dealing with Covid-19: Understanding the policy choices*. BIS Bulletins No 19.

Boyer, R. (2020). *Les capitalismes à l'épreuve de la pandémie*. La Découverte.

Bykova, A. (2021). *Sectoral data underlines differentiated COVID-19 economic impact on CESEE*. WIIW.

Delteil, V. (2018, Autumn). Capitalismes dépendants» d'Europe centrale et orientale: pièges de la dépendance externe et instrumentations domestiques. *Revue de la régulation* [online], 24 | 2nd semester.

Eichenbaum, M., Rebelo, S., & Trabandt, M. (2020). *The macroeconomics of epidemics* (NBER Working Paper No. 26882).

English, B., Forbes, K., & Ubide, A. (Eds.). (2021). *Monetary policy and Central Banking in the Covid era*. CEPR Press. https://voxeu.org/content/monetary-policy-and-central-banking-covid-era

IMF. (2021a). *Policy responses to Covid-19*. https://www.imf.org/en/Topics/imf-and-covid19/Policy-Responses-to-COVID-19K

IMF. (2021b). *Annual report on exchange arrangements and exchange restrictions 2020*.https://www.elibrary.imf.org/view/books/012/29310-9781513556567-en/29310-9781513556567-en-book.xml

Johns Hopkins Coronavirus Resource Center. (2020). *Mortality analyses*. https://coronavirus.jhu.edu/data/mortality

Love, J. (1996). *Crafting the third world: Theorizing underdevelopment in Rumania and Brazil*. Stanford University Press.

Magnin, E., & Nenovsky, N. (2022). Balkan monetary dependence during the XIXth and XXth centuries. *Economic Alternatives*, (2), 171–200.

Nenovsky, N., & Torre, D. (2015). Productivity based protectionism: A Marxian reconstruction of Mihail Manoilescu's theory. *Journal of Economic Issues*, *49*(3), 772–786.

Nenovsky, N., & Torre, D. (2018). Manoilescu's approach of the "losses of trade": A Ricardian interpretation. *Economic Alternatives*, *1*, 49–54.

Nenovsky, N., & Rizopoulos, Y. (2003). Extreme monetary regime change. Evidence from currency board introduction in Bulgaria. *Journal of Economic Issues, 37*(4), 909–941.

Nenovsky, N., & Rizopoulos, Y. (2004). Peut-on mesurer le changement institutionnel du régime monétaire? *Revue D'économie Financière, 75*, 17–36.

Sahling, C., Nenovsky, N., & Chobanov, P. (2021). Diversity of monetary regimes and reactions to the pandemic crisis: Bulgaria, Romania, and Serbia compared. In P. Kostis (Ed.), *Bridging microeconomics and macroeconomics and the effects on economic development and growth* (pp. 276–296). IGI Global.

Wisła, R., & Dykas, P. (2022). *The socioeconomic impact of COVID-19 on Eastern European Countries*. Routledge.

Index

E. Magnin and N. Nenovsky, *Diversity of Capitalism in Central and Eastern Europe*, https://doi.org/10.1007/978-3-031-04950-7

FSC
www.fsc.org
MIX
Papier | Fördert gute Waldnutzung
FSC® C083411

Kolibri 360 GmbH
Ferdinand-Jühlke-Straße 7
99095 Erfurt, Deutschland
produktsicherheit@kolibri360.de